Buried Truths

Fraud & Corruption Hidden in Corporate America

Written By

Robert Crook CPA, CFF

Published by Franklin Publishers
Printed in the United States of America

For permissions, inquiries, or additional copies, contact:
Franklin Publishers
www.franklinpublishers.com

Preface

This book is for those who feel paralyzed by fear, unable to move forward or see what lies beyond it. Fear can be a powerful barrier, keeping you from discovering who you truly are, what the world holds for you, and the impact you can have on others. I once had the privilege of working with a wise woman who often reminded me that life is about the journey, not the destination. Her words stuck with me, especially during the times I leaned on the kindness of others just to make it through another day.

From my childhood to my adulthood, trauma was a constant shadow until I finally sought help. Therapy and the support I found in Al-Anon and Alcoholics Anonymous became my lifeline. The principles I learned there—trust God, clean house, and help others—are simple in theory but transformative in practice. Taking life one day at a time changed everything for me. It wasn't an overnight transformation, but once I embraced those steps, I discovered a freedom I'd never known. Fear no longer had a hold on me.

My journey has spanned more than 40 years, beginning with my first job as a young auditor and CPA at Arthur Andersen in downtown St. Louis. Through all the highs and lows, I've come to understand the power of living for today—not being consumed by the past or obsessed with the future. This book is a reflection of that journey and the lessons learned along the way, living life on life's terms.

Table of Contents

CHAPTER 1

How did I get here?

It has been over seven years since I left my last job in Corporate America. I had been a Chief Audit Executive for one of the largest conglomerates in the United States, Loews Corporation. I worked in the insurance, tobacco, offshore drilling, natural gas pipeline and hotel industries for more than a decade. I worked for historical figures and billionaires. I began writing this book after my last journey in Corporate America. I have spent over 40 years as a Certified Public Accountant, an Auditor, Controller, Chief Financial Officer, Chief Audit Executive and Candidate for US Congress with the last name of Crook. My last name, Crook, is an oxymoron as I am a whistleblower who reports the truth. I have a gift for finding fraud, discovering nefarious acts and criminal activity, and spotting dishonest people. Some would call it a curse, but to me, it was what

I did, and it came naturally. This book is about my story. In some cases, the names have been changed, and yes, to protect the innocent.

I have learned through therapy and self-help that trauma and the resulting chaos and insanity that I survived growing up in an alcoholic family of six children prepared me to work in dysfunctional and chaotic work environments and thrive. I am a middle child. We moved every three years, all over the United States, because of my dad's job. My dad was an alcoholic with an explosive personality disorder. All six of us are adult children of an alcoholic. This diagnosis helps to explain how I react to people, places, and things. When dad came home from work, we hid. On most days, he was explosive and angry. He always had a horrible day, and someone was going to pay for it. Dad yelled at us, demeaned us, and beat us. He had an abusive narcissistic personality that played all of us against one another, a defense mechanism so we would not gang up on him. This narcissistic abuse is something that has kept our family separated many years later. As my dad tells it, the stress of his work as an officer and troubleshooter for Monsanto led to his explosive eruptions on all of us. The stress of commuting, the stress of finding problems that needed to be fixed that no one would deal with, and the stress of coming home to a houseful of six children who needed his attention. Dad was exhausted by the end of the day and could not give any of us his time. I believe that he did the best that he could. Our home was a chaotic place. At least once a month, someone was rushed to the emergency room for a broken bone or stitches. Our Mom was a super mom. She did all she could to keep the family together as we moved from state to state, like Army brats, but instead brats of Corporate America. I learned to become a people pleaser in order to survive.

My experiences in corporate America were equally chaotic. As a CPA and corporate officer, I learned that members of the Boards of Directors are hand-picked because they are someone the Chief Executive Officer (CEO) or owner feels can help them, have connections, and they can trust to support them. In some cases, there is nepotism, and it is not hidden but overtly practiced. My experience is that many directors are hand-picked to vote the way the CEO wants them to. It is almost always about connections and what they can do for the Company. As outlandish as it may sound, hiring a childhood friend of the CEO to be the Audit Committee chairperson happens more frequently than you would think.

After working closely with a dozen NYSE Audit Committees, I rarely found that audit committee members possessed the skills, experience, and training necessary to execute their required duties. As an example, Dr. Henry Kissinger was a member of the R.H. Macy & Co., Inc. (Macy's) Audit Committee. Dr Kissinger was a diplomat and a politician with lots of outside connections. He rarely understood the accounting information that was given to him that he was required to vote on or approve. In my earliest days as a Senior Manager on the audit of Macy's,

I recall that it took the external auditors three different attempts to explain to Dr. Henry Kissinger what inventory shortage was. At Macy's, there was a whole lot of shortage. In the end it was an exercise in futility. He could not comprehend it. What we should have used was an example from the Vietnam War that he might have understood. (Something like, if 100 boys go to war, only 50 come back; that is a shortage.)

My experience is that Boards of Directors and the Chief Executive Officer (CEO) do what is good for them, not so much for the shareholders or stakeholders. The saying goes, the truth will always set you free… Is this true in today's America? Does everyone who leaves a job as a former officer or trusted servant sign a non-disclosure agreement and receive a payoff? Why does your former employer not want you to disclose what really went on in their Company? If a former employee is subpoenaed by the Securities Exchange Commission (SEC) or other governmental agency about what happened when you were an employee, you are required to tell the truth under oath, even if your non-disclosure agreement says otherwise. Will this ever change? What, if any, responsibility does the SEC have to ensure that crimes committed in a public company are properly adjudicated? Only if material? In cases of Senior management committing fraud or directing manipulation of accounting records, it does need to be material to have a devastating effect on the tone and the culture of the Company.

I have witnessed some of the largest business failures in America. I have watched countless companies fail. I spent the first 20 years of my career working in the retail sector, primarily in Department Stores. I watched all the mergers, acquisitions, and the final ruination of local department stores throughout the US. Probably the most recognizable failure was R.H. Macy & Co., Inc. (Macy's). By that time, things at Macy's had collapsed around me. It was 1993, and I was 32 years old. I had been the outside accountant for Macy's and a senior officer in corporate offices and in two of their largest subsidiaries. After just 7 years, I was a seasoned veteran of corporate chaos, especially in retail and apparel companies. I had seen more insanity, earned more money, and accomplished more in those seven years than my father, who had spent 40 years as the Controller of the Monsanto Chemical Company. Rapid change, international wars, and bankruptcy create instability and are environments where fraud can flourish and go undetected. All these factors were present at Macy's. Fraud occurred because of it. The tone, good or bad, is set from the top of an organization. If the Board, CEO, or the person in charge only cares about their own well-being and not that of the Company and its stakeholders, it creates an environment where people want to get even with the Company. Employees that steal rationalize their behavior, as they "deserve it" because they were mistreated or underpaid. If there are no systems or controls in place to prevent theft, it presents the opportunity to steal and not get caught. Finally, the third component of fraud is financial pressure or stress. Macy's was not able to pay its bills as they came due. All three of these factors were present at Macy's and in a large portion of the retail sector from 1985 through 2000.

In 1993, I took a job as Controller of the most exclusive high-end retailer in the United States, Bergdorf Goodman. I knew the Chief Executive Officer (CEO) as the company had been a client of mine since my days at Deloitte & Touche. After three years of troubleshooting, cutting costs, and moving back-office operations from New York to Dallas, where their sister company, Neiman Marcus, was headquartered, I was let go. This was not an amicable parting. I was required to investigate my boss, the CEO, based on allegations of a kickback scheme. What I found was much worse. The CEO tried to blackmail me into working with his longtime corrupt team. I would not play ball or participate. My reputation was smeared by the CEO, and I fought back by reporting the fraud & corruption in the Company. And I ultimately settled with my employer. As my longtime boss, rabbi, and mentor from Macy's, Don Eugene, said to me at the time, you cannot let these people get away with this. They did not. This was an extremely painful thing for me to go through. I prided myself on my integrity, ethics and my retail knowledge and expertise, both operationally and from an accounting perspective. Less than two years after leaving Bergdorf Goodman, the entire long-time Bergdorf Goodman executive team was eliminated. This did give me some sense of justice. But how many others suffered the wrath of these people and did not get compensated, and were left in a hopeless place? Do these CEOs and Boards ever get what they deserve? Does karma ever play out? I believe it does and have witnessed it. It just takes time, not in our time but in the universe's time. I also believe ethics and morality are instilled in us at a young age. Factors such as nepotism and greed make it almost impossible to ensure ethics and morals are followed in a public Company.

As I look back on those early years navigating the chaos of Corporate America, I can see how my personal experiences and professional challenges were deeply intertwined. The lessons I learned—both from my tumultuous upbringing and the corporate boardrooms— shaped my ability to uncover fraud and face the unrelenting pressures of dysfunctional workplaces. It wasn't just about numbers and audits; it was about understanding people, motives, and the intricate web of decisions that lead to corruption. In the chapters ahead, I'll take you deeper into the world of retail accounting and fraud, sharing the stories, lessons, and battles that defined my career and tested my integrity at every turn.

CHAPTER 2

My First Encounters with retail accounting & fraud

Looking back in the rear-view mirror about this part of my life and what I would do differently is easy today. But in August 1996, I was in deep depression. For the 2nd time in three years, I had lost a job as an officer of a major retailer. I had done my job in an exemplary fashion, been promoted, and found problems and fixed them, saving my employers and clients tens of millions of dollars, hundreds of multiples of what I was paid. Why was I let go? The answer was simple. I found fraud, corruption and stealing, and those above me were afraid that they may be exposed next. I was not afraid to expose anyone or anything. I always told the truth. I learned from a young age that hard work and telling the truth are important in life. I have always believed that the truth will prevail, eventually.

My ability to find fraud and to work in chaotic places, like Macy's post-LBO and during the bankruptcy, was something I learned how to navigate because of the trauma I endured growing up. I gravitated to chaos. To me, it was normal. It was what I was accustomed to. Trauma is defined as a physical, cognitive, and emotional response to a harmful or life-threatening event or circumstance. It can cause lasting adverse effects on a person's mental health, physical health, emotional health, social well-being, and spiritual well-being. The effects of trauma manifested itself in my personality and in my work ethic, as I am an adult child of an alcoholic.

I was born in 1961, the 3rd of six children, in a Roman Catholic family. My father was an accountant for Monsanto Chemical Company in St. Louis, Mo. My mother was a stay-at-home mom. My earliest memories were of my grandparents' farms, where they raised Black Angus cattle and grew soybeans. While they were both farmers, my grandparents were as different as my parents, like night and day. I learned from my family the importance of hard work and telling the truth. My mother was warm and outgoing, and our primary caregiver and my dad worked and was never home. I do not have a lot of happy memories of my childhood. There were six of us (five boys and one girl). My Mom made all our clothes and cooked every meal. She was a super Mom. She did a job like no other Mom I knew. My mother taught me that all of us have our own free will, given to us by God, to choose right from wrong. I have tried to follow this lesson throughout my life. I will always be grateful to my mother for this. It was this upbringing and circumstances that taught me to work hard and never give up.

Because of my dad's job, we moved from place to place from the time I was born to the time I graduated from High School, five different times. We lived in suburban St. Louis twice, in suburban New Jersey, outside Dayton, Ohio, and in Tuscaloosa, AL. In all the places we lived, our family was accepted into the community except for one. Moving to Alabama in 1976, our family was referred to as the damned Yankees. I never knew I was a Yankee or a Buckeye. I just thought I was a teenager who was weary of moving and was in my second Junior High School, about to enter High School. If the moving around was not chaotic enough, our father was an alcoholic who was very abusive to all of us, particularly me, because I was gay, told the truth, and was not afraid to hide from it.

While in college in St. Louis, I took a job at a local department store, Stix, Baer & Fuller (Stix). I learned about point-of-sale registers, mark-ups, mark-downs, mark-up cancels, mark-down cancels, inventory shortages, cash register shortages, store security, and everything that happened on the selling floor related to checking and marking merchandise. I was fascinated by retail accounting and how this all got recorded into the retail stock ledger. I also learned about theft and fraud at Stix. There was theft of merchandise daily by gangs from North and East St. Louis and theft from the cash register by sales associates. The gangs would come into the store, grab a rack of clothes, and run out the nearest door. There were also professional thieves who strapped large boxes to their stomachs. Over the box, they wore maternity clothes, appearing to be pregnant. This was the perfect place to hide clothes or anything else they were stealing. I learned how to work with store security and found out how to spot fraudsters and theft rings. The summer of 1982 was my Junior Year of college. I interviewed for an internship in the Controller's office at Stix with the Controller, Mark S. Sellers. I thought I had a good interview, but as it turned out, I did not get the job. A few weeks passed, and I heard from my friend in security that Mr. Sellers had been taken out of the building in handcuffs that day. At that point, I did not feel so bad about not getting the job. Exactly what Mark Sellers had done to have him handcuffed and removed from the building was never disclosed in public. This would not be my last encounter with Mark S. Sellers and the lessons of karma.

I graduated from College in May 1983, Magna Cum Laude. I took the weekend off after graduation and started working the next Monday at Arthur Andersen's (AA & Co's) St. Louis office. One of the first large-scale frauds I was exposed to was the Defense Dept. overbilling scheme by General Dynamics. General Dynamics had billed the US government for $640 toilet seats on Fighter planes the government had purchased. All the work papers of the General Dynamics audit for the prior 10 years were held in the St. Louis office of AA & Co. and had to be photocopied to prepare for a criminal trial. That summer, in between making copies of work papers, running errands, and working on audits, I studied for the CPA exam, which I passed a year later. While in the St. Louis office of AA & Co. I worked on manufacturing clients, hospitals, and department stores, notably the May Dept. Stores Company.

While at Touche Ross (later known as Deloitte & Touche) in the late 80's we were frequently asked to opine on irregular retail accounting and fraud. We were seen as the experts by the Securities & Exchange Commission (SEC). Some of the examples I remember from the government's case against Crazy Eddie still stick with me today. Crazy Eddie (Eddie Antar) was indicted by the SEC and the Southern District of NY for defrauding investors out of more than $100 million dollars. The accounting and financial statements of Crazy Eddie were fraudulently prepared. The financial statements filed with the SEC showed a profitable operation. This was not the case; the Company was losing money. Inventory was the main source of the fraud. If you increase inventory, you increase profits. A physical inventory count is a way for inventory to be validated for audit purposes. All physical inventory should be counted at the same time to prevent manipulation of the records. Crazy Eddie moved inventory between stores and counted the same inventory in multiple locations on multiple days, having the effect of substantially increasing inventory balances. This does not seem like a complicated scheme to uncover, but their auditors did not find it. The electronics business was highly competitive, and the margins were very low, yet somehow Crazy Eddie had the lowest retail prices, and they were "insane," according to his advertising campaign. What was insane was how gross margin was manipulated by creating fraudulent chargebacks to electronics vendors. These fraudulent chargebacks were hung up in the accounts payable trial balance for years. No one ever questioned all these debit balances in the accounts payable trial balance, and whether they were valid and collectible, they were not. In the case of Crazy Eddie there was an overpowering boss who directed the accounting fraud and the fictitious accounting. Without a competent audit committee, external auditors, and independent governance, fraud was easily concocted and not detected for years.

Because of my experience at Stix, I was assigned to the May Company audit. The CFO of the May Company was a man named Jerry Loeb, and the CEO was David Farrell. Many who worked for them saw them as real-life evil emperors of the dark side, like Darth Vader. AA & Co. ran merger scenarios (war games) for the May Company. I was in the office late one night in the Spring of 1985. I was one of the few who were trusted to deliver a printout of one of the war games to the corner of Olive & 8th St. I was there when Jerry Loeb's driver pulled up in a dark limo with tinted windows. The passenger side window pulled down, and Jerry Loeb asked me for a password. I told him I did not have a password; he asked me my name and who I worked for. I told him AA & Co. and my name. The driver reached out across the seat, pulled down the front side window, and grabbed the package from me. Both windows closed, and the car drove off as mysteriously as it had arrived. The next morning, I told the manager on the account about the encounter, and he laughed. That's Jerry Loeb. I asked who the target was, and he told me ADG, that being Associated Dry Goods Corporation, the parent company of Stix, Baer & Fuller, Lord & Taylor, Caldor, Robinson's, Goldwater's Hahne's, and over a dozen other dept. stores throughout the US.

The lessons I learned during those early encounters with retail accounting and fraud would become the foundation of my career, shaping not only my skills but also my perspective on the corporate world. From spotting thieves on the selling floor to uncovering multimillion-dollar frauds, I began to understand the patterns of dishonesty and the systems that allowed it to thrive. But these experiences were only the beginning. As I moved forward in my career, the stakes grew higher, the schemes more elaborate, and the challenges more personal. What lay ahead would test everything I thought I knew about integrity, resilience, and the cost of telling the truth.

CHAPTER 3

If you Can Make it there, you can make it Anywhere

In September of 1985, I moved to New York City and transferred with AA & Co. to their New York office. The New York office of AA & Co. was not the same place I had left in St. Louis. In the St Louis office, I knew everyone, and we took direction from headquarters in Chicago. The New York Office of AA & Co. was a renegade office and was not run well. The audits that I was assigned to had no prior year files or work papers. How was an audit done if there were no work papers to substantiate the work? I was not happy there, so I interviewed at Touche Ross & Co. (Touche), one of the eight big firms. I started at Touche just before Thanksgiving. New York City was an enormous change from St. Louis. It was the city that never sleeps and was living in the wild west village at 95 Horatio St. Today, this is where the Highline begins. The new Whitney Museum is behind my old Apt. Building. Back in the mid-80s, it was on the border of the meatpacking district, and it was like Halloween 365 days a year there, filled with prostitutes and drug addicts dressed up in clothes that looked more like costumes. 95 Horatio, the West Coast Building, was a doorman building with lofts and apartments. It was one of the few available places that I could find to live in, coming from St. Louis. It was my first NYC apartment. People in the building were nice enough in the lobby of the building, but once you got off the elevator it was a completely different story. There was no eye contact with your neighbors. As they walked from the elevator to their apartment, they would look down at the floor, hurriedly fumbling to find their door keys. They would open their apartment door and close the door behind them as fast as they could. No chit-chat, no neighborly pleasantries, just hardened people living a reclusive life. It was like this the entire time that I lived at 95 Horatio St.

The first audit I was assigned to at Touche was Associated Dry Goods Corporation (ADG), as the in-charge Senior. I remember telling the Partner in charge of the New York office that ADG was going to be acquired by the May Company. He looked at me like, what does this kid from St. Louis know? He did not even give me a chance to explain myself. This was not the last time I would speak about this to the boss. I really loved living in the city. I was 24 years old and worked 60 to 70 hours a week. After the audit of ADG was over, I got sucked into the fever of the Macy's Leveraged Buy-out (LBO). Since I was not from New York, had lived in other parts of the country, and worked on the sales floor, I understood the locations where Macy's and their subsidiaries had stores and its customers. I worked with the Touche consultants on sales projections and challenged the reasonability of departmental & new store sales projections. In June of 1986, I was awoken at 6:00 am on a Monday morning by the managing partner of the NY office of Touche. He wanted to know everything I knew about May Company's acquisition of ADG. A hostile takeover was being launched that morning. Soon after The May Company acquired ADG in a hostile takeover, from that moment on, I was taken seriously by the firm.

Macy's Leveraged Buy Out (LBO) was the first of its kind in many respects. The first of many to follow, the first of many to later file for bankruptcy protection, ultimately led to a complete takeover and turnaround by its chief competitor, Federated Department Stores. Both Macy's and Federated were my clients. Federated had a January year-end, and Macy's had a July year-end, so I could work on both jobs. Clients are all about relationships. My relationship at Macy's was very strong with the Controller, Don Eugene. At Federated, I knew the Controller, Jack Brown, but I did not have as much contact as I did with Don.

In January of 1988, Campeau Corp, backed by First hostile tender offer for Federated Dept. stores. This was in the middle of the yearend audit. I was the Senior Audit

Manager on the Federated audit for the firm. Two years earlier, Campeau had acquired Allied Stores Corp. in a similar LBO. The Allied LBO was not successful. Allied was selling off assets to support its exorbitant debt load and interest payments. Campeau needed another deal to help him get out of his Allied negative cash flow position. The bid for Federated became a Ponzi scheme, the assets from Federated were needed to help pay down the debt from the ill-fated Allied deal. The Partners at Touche knew this and issued a qualified opinion on the financial statements of Federated Department Stores. A qualified opinion meant that the financial statements could not be relied upon. They knew the resulting combination with Allied would render Federated insolvent, and it was doubtful that the combined company could continue as a going concern. In fact, the SEC required a solvency letter to be issued before Campeau could close on the Federated acquisition, funded by junk bonds, and a $1 billion line of credit (financed by First Boston) to be rolled into junk bonds. First Boston, the firm that would make 10 million dollars by underwriting the deal, issued the credit line and the solvency letter. This appeared to be a conflict of interest, but the deal closed, and the demise of Federated was history. This was my first understanding of conflict of interest and a real-life Ponzi scheme. It happened right in front of my eyes. Touche, though, did the right thing by issuing a qualified opinion on Federated Dept. stores and lost the audit. This was the beginning of the end of Touche's dominance in the retail accounting and consulting business. More than 10 offices of the firm worked on the audit of Federated. The same thing happened when Associated Dry Goods was acquired by the May Company.

My memories of the Controller of Federated, Jack Brown, ended in March of 1988 when I landed late one night at Teterboro on the Federated jet. Jack went on to meet with investment bankers reviewing bids from Campeau for properties and stores to be sold, and I went on to meet folks from Macy's and Loews (Larry Tisch's Company) at Ed Finklestein's townhouse on the upper eastside, who were preparing a competing bid for Federated. Ed held the power to vote on all shares of Macy's, even though management owned the shares and Ed was King.

Macy's had several high-profile board members, including Larry Tisch from Loews, Sidney J. Weinberg (Jim) from Goldman Sachs, Al Taubman, the Shopping Center Developer, Michael Price, the Hedge Fund Owner, and Sir Run Run Shaw, a Hong Kong entertainment mogul. Ed Finklestein added these people to the board so they could help him, instead they ended up killing him off. Out of the box, Macy's had a successful LBO, so successful that the Board felt they needed to take a run at Federated as the white knight to help it from being bought out by Campeau Corp. Larry Tisch felt it was Macy's name that would have great marketing recognition across the US. Macy's, though, ended up with the West Coast dept. Store operations of Federated that included Bullock's, Bullock's Wilshire, and I. Magnin and an additional $565 million in debt. What happened to both companies exemplifies what happened during the late eighties as far as greed amongst investment bankers, egregious amounts of junk bond debt, fraudulent conveyance of transactions that were insolvent from their inception, and the resulting bankruptcies that attorneys, accountants, and their advisors fed off. It was a vicious cycle of greed and fraud.

Macy's junk bonds and related interest put a tremendous cash flow burden on Macy's. Macy's was forced to sell off its credit card receivables to General Electric to generate cash needed to repay debt maturities that were coming due. The banks required more financial controls to be installed at the great and powerful R. H. Macy & Co., Inc. Many of its systems were still running on IBM punch cards and Fortran and Cobol mainframe programs. Ed and Macy's board recruited a computer and finance-oriented guy to appease the banks. His name was Myron Ullman III, "Mike" or as his predecessor and the waiters in the 13th-floor executive dining room called him, the Small Mouth. Mike did not speak loudly, as did the merchant princes that surrounded him, and he took small bites from his food, hence the name small mouth. He fouled everybody as he took large bites out of those he encountered who did not see things the way he did. He brought in many henchmen and women to execute his plans for the decimation of the Company.

As my career in New York unfolded, I began to see how the greed, power plays, and conflicts of interest within corporate America could bring even the largest and most established companies to their knees. The lessons I learned during the Macy's and Federated battles, the high-stakes world of leveraged buyouts, and my firsthand exposure to Ponzi-like schemes taught me the true cost of unchecked ambition and financial manipulation. But this was just the beginning. In the chapters ahead, I'll delve deeper into the players, decisions, and moments that would further test my resolve and challenge my understanding of ethics in an industry driven by profit at any cost.

CHAPTER 4

Working in Beautiful Downtown Newark

I began my job as Administrator of Accounts Payable, Sales Audit, and Expense Payable in beautiful downtown Newark in the Fall of 1990. I can remember my first day in the old Bamberger's building like it was yesterday. I was 29 years old. I had over 600 employees reporting to me. Arriving on the 6th floor in the elevator, I remember being in the back of a packed elevator car and hearing staff talking about the new Administrator who was starting that day, a man with the last name of Crook. I heard one person say, "I wonder how long this one will last." While I thought I was invincible, this was a great question. The average tenure of my predecessors in Newark was 18 months. The prior administrator, nicknamed by my boss as the 'Hummel Figure' (because he looked like one), had a heart attack while on the job due to the stress and chaos. In Newark, Macy's ran two separate companies' back-office systems as one, mostly manually. Fires and knifings inside the building were not uncommon, and we had at least a year's backlog of unanswered vendor correspondence in the accounts payable department. I worked 60 to 70 hours a week and left the building by car late at night. The Newark police told me to not stop at any red lights after dark as it was a dangerous place and to just run them. I think it was as dangerous inside the building as it was on the streets of Newark at that time.

Mike Ullman's first new hire was a new Chief Financial Officer (CFO), who was a bankruptcy expert, hired from Salomon Bros., where they had cut their teeth on the bankruptcy of US Steel. The CFO was tall and had a gawky and manly look about her, not feminine. Many described her as looking like a truck driver dressed in a Chanel suit. The CFO had little knowledge of the world of retailing or fashion. Don Eugene, my friend and boss, affectionately referred to her as the B.O.B. (the beast of Belsen or the bitch of Buchenwald, whichever one you preferred). The B.O.B. was a hired hand, had killer instincts, had no fondness for the Macy's of old but was concerned about remaking Macy's and did not care who they pissed off. The B.O.B. had no appreciation for the creative side of the business, the merchants, or the visual merchandisers. They had no interpersonal skills as far as dealing with customers, public relations or store publicity. The B.O.B. was there to improve the earnings before interest taxes, depreciation, and amortization (EBITDA) that was it. My encounters with the B.O.B. were not frequent, as I was a loyalist to both Don and Ed, and they knew not to speak to me. Macy's was a very tough place to work, and Don and Ed ruled there for almost 4 decades. At the time of the LBO, Don, while Controller, held the second highest number of shares of R.H. Macy & Co., Inc. common stock. Ed held the most shares. Don and Ed had the support of the rank and file. At this point in my career, whether as an auditor with Deloitte & Touche or as a newly hired Administrator of the back offices in the Bamberger's building in Newark, I was in the protective care of Don Eugene and Ed Finkelstein. So long as Ed was King, all was good.

Within my first week on the job, I learned of the first of many fraud schemes operating in my dept. My secretary alerted me to a phone call from "Matty, the Horse." I grew up in the Midwest, was naïve, and had never encountered a mobster. Mr. Matty the Horse's real name was Matthew Ianniello, a reputed organized crime figure. I opened one of my desk draws, and there was a contract between Macy's and Mr. Ianniello for all of Macy's salvage merchandise. Macy's accepted returns from customers back then, no questions asked. Much of this merchandise was damaged and could not be easily resold. It was referred to as salvaged merchandise. At this same time, almost daily, I received calls from other outside vendors who wanted to buy our salvage merchandise, but Mr. Matty the Horse's contract was for less than half the amount that others had offered.

I sent a copy of the contract to Don in Herald Square. Within an hour, I was visited by local investigators from the FBI in Newark. It seems that the address on the contract was an empty lot in Kearny, NJ, and all the Company records for the transactions and files had gone missing. Yes, the files of all the transactions had been destroyed, which is usually a good sign that something nefarious was up. The contract, though, had been signed by a former officer of Macy's. Macy's tried to nullify the contract due to its non-advantageous nature, but a Federal Judge upheld the contract since it was signed by an officer of Macy's Northeast. (Others assumed there was a kickback scheme, but there were no records to prove it.) I received death threats for 6 months after this report was made, and my home in Sleepy Hollow was monitored by police and security. This experience ingrained in me why anonymous reporting and protecting a whistle-blower is important. I was an innocent employee, just trying to do my job. What was the point of trying to scare or frighten me? What was discovered could not be undone.

Each day in the Newark building was an adventure. The old Bamberger's building, like Herald Square, was a behemoth of a building that sat on an entire city block in downtown Newark, next to the Prudential building. The Bamberger's building in Newark was a landmark, with a tearoom and restaurant for shoppers. Back in the day, shoppers would travel by bus or train from the suburbs and spend an entire day shopping in downtown Newark. The old executive offices were palatial, with a daybed and a shower in the former CEO's office. There was also a "tap room" in the building that Louis Bamberger had built for his employees to use, I assume, after the end of the workday. Those days of shopping in downtown Newark were long gone. The selling space in the building had been reduced to only two floors. This left a cavernous building with a lot of empty offices. The data center for all East Coast operations of Macy's was also housed in the old Bamberger's building. When the decision was made to outsource the credit card operations to General Electric, there were fires set in the data center. These were assumed to be disgruntled employees who were losing their jobs and wanted to sabotage the migration.

The woman who ran the check sorting machine for accounts payable, Monica, was regularly drunk, and vendors would ply her with whiskey to gain her favor. Those vendors that gave her a pint of whiskey could come and pick up their checks (which were, in most cases, over a million dollars). All other checks were sent through regular mail. This is how things had operated in Newark for decades before I got there. This processing and the mailing of the checks changed after I had been transferred to the West Coast. I was told by Don that prior to Macy's filing for bankruptcy, vendor checks were sent to the Treasury Dept. in Herald Square for distribution. It was here that staff were instructed to defame the checks before they were mailed. Pin holes were placed in the micro-encoded number (MICR) on the bottom of the check. These pinholes prevented the bank from reading the MICR numbers and rendered the checks invalid when the bank tried to deposit them. Prior to a company filing for bankruptcy, lots of shenanigans occur. This was just one of many.

One of the most colorful vendor meetings I ever had while at Macy's was with the people from Revlon. Revlon had been bought out by Ron Perelman in the late eighties, and we had vendor correspondence disputes with them going back over 6 years. The cosmetics business in a department store is not an easy business. The vendor must sell enough merchandise to cover the demonstrator's payroll, advertising, and any samples or promotional costs that are given to customers. Revlon was a line that had fallen out of favor on the main floor at Macy's as it was trading up to brands like Lancôme and Estee Lauder. Perelman wanted to keep the merchandise in Macy's, and Finklestein wanted it out. Little did I know, I was in the middle of a fight that caused Macy's to close Revlon from all its stores in the US. I had been set up to assist in the endeavor of getting rid of Revlon by orchestrating this meeting. Macy's Northeast records indicated that Revlon owed us a little over $2 million. Revlon's records indicated that Macy's owed Revlon a little over $2 million, a $4 million difference.

I agreed to meet with Revlon Senior Management at a settlement conference in Herald Square to see if we could iron things out. We had Rosemarie Bravo, DMM, Bob Chavez, Buyer, and Don in the meeting. The Controller from Revlon attended, as did their head of credit. From the beginning, things did not go well. The folks from Revlon dropped the F-bomb on the buyers and merchants from Macy's. My staff and I just sat there and listened cordially for an hour. Rosemarie Bravo and Bob Chavez got up and walked out of the meeting as did my boss. The people from Revlon would not stop yelling, and after an hour, Macy's Security escorted them out of the building. While I had grown up in a chaotic home with yelling and screaming, I had never seen this type of behavior in a professional work setting. I left the meeting and went to catch the train back to my office in Newark when I got a message from Don to meet him in Mr. Finklestein's office on the 13th floor. While I had met Mr. Finklestein on many different occasions, I had never been to his office. He had an enormous private garden terrace, and his office was palatial. As I entered Ed's office, Don was sitting across from Ed, and behind him were Rosemarie Bravo and Bob Chavez, standing. Don and Ed waved me in to sit across from Ed. Ed took a call from Ron Perelman as I sat there, stunned. Perelman told Ed that "Crook" and his people had treated his employees badly and abused them, and he demanded that Macy's pay Revlon the $2 million they owed Revlon. Rosemarie and Bob Chavez spoke up and told Mr. Finklestein and Mr. Perelman that this was not true, that Mr. Crook and his people were professional and withstood insults and slurs that no one else would have taken. Ed then abruptly took over the conversation and told Ron Perelman, "As I am speaking, each and every Macy's store across the United States is packing up Revlon merchandise and awaiting instructions for it to be returned to either Revlon or outside jobbers."

"If we receive a check from Revlon, we will send it back to Revlon. Otherwise, we will sell it to the highest bidder." Representatives from the legal dept. then entered Mr. Finklestein's office, and I left. To this day, I have never met a tougher negotiator than Ed Finklestein; he was one of a kind and the last of the great merchant princes. In the end, the merchandise was sold off to jobbers, and Revlon was no longer carried in any Macy's stores.

While at Macy's Northeast in Newark, the painful reality of antiquated systems and processes affected my job and my people daily. Mike Ullman was an advocate for change and modernization and had a background in systems and computers, particularly IBM and Federated Dept. store's systems group, named SABRE, headquartered in Norcross, GA. Macy's had tried for years to modernize its systems and had failed. The labor costs and the lack of data in the new world of SKUs, EDI, and data mining kept Macy's from succeeding, especially with its extreme debt load and high junk bond interest payments. The Board of Directors approved the outsourcing of all systems to SABRE. This, on the surface, seemed to be a conflict of interest as Federated competed with Macy's in every market, and they were in the middle of Chapter 11 restructuring due to an ill-fated takeover by Bob Campeau. Mike, though, convinced the board that this was the only way to stave off Macy's bankruptcy. Macy's Northeast was the first division to implement the new systems, and the epicenter of the systems' conversion was my dept. in downtown Newark. We started working on the conversion in January of 1991, and we completed it by August 1991. The folks from SABRE had completed similar conversions at over 10 other divisions of Federated but had never seen such success as we had in Newark from a technical standpoint. There was one problem, though: our labor force. We had a union in Newark, the old Bamberger's union, that had bumping rights. Due to the automation of punched cards and manual entry to automated online systems, our head counts were reduced. A WARN notice was issued by Human Resources due to the severity of the layoffs throughout the Company. A WARN notice is required to be issued when more than 100 employees are terminated. Because of the bumping rights provision in the union contract, the folks we were required to keep were those that had the longest service to the Company. This meant that 150 employees, in most cases over 60 years of age, were guaranteed jobs. These employees were not able to adjust to the new online systems environment, and the Company made the decision to close the Newark facility and transition the positions to a new shared service center outside of Atlanta, GA. Many of the managers and supervisors from Newark were offered jobs in Atlanta. I, on the other hand, was promoted to Vice President of Control Operations of Macy's West and sent to San Francisco to start the 2nd conversion to SABRE.

My time in Newark taught me that even in the face of chaos, outdated systems, and impossible odds, it's possible to achieve remarkable results with perseverance, innovation, and a strong team. From uncovering mob ties to navigating volatile vendor disputes, I saw firsthand the darker side of corporate operations and the resilience required to confront it. Yet, Newark was just one chapter in a larger story. As the company shifted focus to modernization and I moved on to new challenges on the West Coast, I knew the lessons I had learned in that beautiful chaos would guide me through even greater battles ahead.

CHAPTER 5

The Wild Wild West

The night before my assignment was to begin on Union Square in San Francisco was the night of the Oakland Hills fire. My plane had landed early in the afternoon, luckily, as San Francisco International was closed due to smoke later that evening. This fire was an omen as to what would happen over the next 9 months. I had rented an apt. on Hyde St. on Russian Hill and remember being awakened to what I thought was the sound of barking dogs. Russian Hill is one of the original 7 named hills of San Francisco. The Cable car line runs on Hyde St. up Russian Hill and ends at the bottom of the hill at Ghirardelli Square, next to Fishermen's Wharf. I later found out at work these were not barking dogs but sea lions down on Fisherman's Wharf. You can take a boy out of the Midwest but cannot take the Midwest out of the boy. I had never seen a sea lion before moving to San Francisco. My upbringing taught me to persevere and stay focused on a job, no matter how difficult it may become. After the Northeast conversion, Macy's split into two separate divisions, Macy's East and Macy's West. I was now part of Macy's West. The management from Macy's South/Bullock's took over the operations and finance control of Macy's East, and a few of us from the East, including my boss Don Eugene, were sent out West. Mike Ullman became Executive Vice President (EVP) and took full control of Corporate, and the B.O.B. became the Chief Financial Officer of all of Macy's. At this point, the invasion of the infidels began to take hold in New York. I remember the first time I saw Mark S. Sellers name as EVP of Macy's East. I asked Don if he knew this man, "Sellers?" He responded that they called him the sphinx because he never spoke in meetings, only privately to the B.O.B. and Mike. I told Don I thought he was the former Controller of Stix, Baer & Fuller, who had been escorted out of the building in handcuffs, although I did not know why. Don, who was a former Head of Security for Macy's, did some digging and told me I was correct. It was from this point forward I knew that dark days were ahead for Macy's.

Ed's son Danny was the Chairman of Macy's California for over 5 years prior to the merger of Bullock's and Macy's California. After the merger, there was no direction given to the staff in Los Angeles at the old Bullock's offices at Hope & 8th St. Danny was comfortable in San Francisco, as was most of his team. They did visit the Los Angeles area stores but never fully embraced their new responsibilities.

Myself, on the other hand, wanted to get my hands on what was happening there at Bullock's in downtown Los Angeles. I was on a shuttle flight every Monday morning and back in San Francisco every Friday night. Bullock's had industry state-of-the-art systems, more advanced in some respects than the SABRE systems we were converting to. For whatever reason, call it a hunch; something drew me to that place. I was hearing stories from the East and from Don about how the Sphinx was building a complex in Herald Square, complete with offices that would allow him to smoke cigars. In turn, Mark Sellers would hold meetings with Merchandise Managers, and he would "smoke them out" to get his way. He would intentionally blow cigar smoke in their faces if they did not do what he wanted them to do. He was a menacing figure who abused his executive privileges and power. He would enlist those who reported to him to act in the same manner. Mark Sellers had created a hostile workplace environment, and it was tolerated.

Preparing for a merger of systems from an accounts payable perspective requires the merger of vendor master files. Both Bullock's and Macy's California had tens of thousands of vendors, and the file was worth well over $200 million. If the wrong vendor was set up or connected in the systems conversion you could wrong pay millions of dollars. Reading the vendor history file and understanding the coding was the most important thing in the systems conversion, especially when connecting the two companies' vendor files. It was during this process in the back-offices of Bullock's in early December 1991 that I found a file with vendor returns in it that looked highly unusual. These returns had been from the prior Spring Season. What the records were indicating were that over $17 million in Men's Suits had been shipped from Bullock's Return Room in La Habra, California, to Macy's South in Atlanta, GA. This seemed very odd. First, that is a lot of suits. If the average Men's Suit cost $150, that means over 113,000 men's suits were transferred. Macy's South and Bullock's were operated as one division prior to the creation of Macy's East and West. Was there a Men's Suit Sale in Atlanta? Were there any Shipping Documents in the La Habra Return to Vendor Room that at least would prove that these suits existed? Was this just a random accounting entry to reduce inventory shortage and improve results as had been done on the books of Crazy Eddie years before? Who would have devised such a scheme? Mark Sellers had built his reputation on reducing inventory shortages and making stores profitable. Was this accounting how he accomplished this? Something was wrong here, and it was serious.

Technically, I reported to the EVP of Macy's West, he was the former Controller of Macy's California. I also reported to Don Eugene, he was President of I. Magnin and in-charge of the SABRE conversion. I rarely spoke to the EVP of the West, I spoke to Don every day, sometimes two or three times a day. I had known Don since I had come to NY, he was my Rabbi. I had a dilemma, who should I report this to? I mentioned the situation to Don, who said to wait until he spoke to Ed Finklestein. At this point, I had no choice but to wait. What I learned from Don was startling. There had been several complaints made against Mark Sellers, and Macy's East Security was investigating allegations of construction fraud and embezzlement from the cash vault in the Main Store on Peachtree St. in Atlanta.

On the night before Christmas Eve 1991, myself and an associate flew from San Francisco to Los Angeles and rented a car. We drove in the dark to the Macy's store in La Habra, passing the Richard Nixon (I am not a crook) library. I had never been to this part of Los Angeles County, and I felt like a detective en route to perform a secret mission to raid a target. I was not afraid. Just before the store closing, we entered the Return to Vendor Room in the La Habra Store. We tried to enter the storage room where documents were stored, and we identified ourselves with our Macy's West employee badges. The employees in the La Habra store would not allow us to enter the facility. It was as if they knew we were coming, and they had been instructed to stonewall us. We went to the store manager's office and requested to enter the facility. We were again denied access. I used the office phone to call Don Eugene in Union Square. He, in turn, called Ed at home in Litchfield Ct. Ed called his son, who in turn called the EVP of the West. The EVP of the West called the store, telling them that they were to give us complete access to the room. We entered the Document Storage Room and asked the custodian of records to give us the Men's Suit Files. The files did not exist. We had gone on a secret mission, the "Raid on La Habra," two days before Christmas and found nothing. This most likely meant accounting shenanigans and manipulations to the tune of $17 million had occurred.

It was at this time; I knew that the EVP of the West was pissed at me. Why didn't I trust him and tell him about the $17 million fraud? I met Don as a client on the audit of Macy's. We became great friends from the beginning. Don was like a father and a role model for me as well. Don was a gay man in a committed relationship for most of his life. I cannot imagine what it was like to be a gay man growing up in the world in the 1950s and 60s and being a manager of a large corporation like Macy's. This was not a known fact; Don was not open or out of the closet. I kept Don's secret confidential. Being gay, I was part of Don's select group of mentees. I was friends with Don through all the insanity of the LBO, Newark conversion, and moving to California. The West EVP should have understood, but he did not. I did not face him again until after the Holidays. Don explained to the West EVP that I had a family emergency, I needed to return home, and my grandfather was ill. I did have to return home. I had to return home to New York the day after Christmas. I stayed at Don's Apt and slept on his couch. The next morning, Dec. 27, 1991, I had a face to face meeting with Deloitte, Cardinal Richelieu (aka Ira Millstein Senior Partner from Weil, Gotschal and Manges), and Larry Tisch (Chairman of Loews Corp.). I was deposed and asked to explain the accounting fraud that I had uncovered in the books of Bullock's relating to $17 million of Men's Suits.

I told them what I knew. They really did not seem

troubled or upset. In retrospect, these two men had been involved in large mergers and takeovers of Corporations worth billions of dollars, and this was small potatoes compared to what these men were accustomed to. I asked Don the next week, "What was the result of the meeting?" Deloitte performed an investigation of their own, and then Ira Millstein agreed not to prosecute Sellers if he resigned from his position and made restitution for the funds he had stolen. The aftermath of this was heartbreaking for many. Mark Sellers had a strong following, like a mobster with cohorts and, yes, henchmen who did his bidding. Some left, others stayed, but it left a bad taste in everyone's mouth, especially for Mike Ullman, who had hired Mark and had high hopes for his success.

Unfortunately, hardened criminals, even white-collar criminals, continue to harm others unless they are brought to justice. In the Spring of 2017, in my office at Loews, I received a call from Don Eugene. Don sent me an email regarding a tragedy that had occurred in Kansas City, MO, that day. It seems that Mark S. Sellers had taken his life. FBI agents had obtained a search warrant that day from a federal magistrate judge. Sellers was not home when the agents showed up at his door, but he sped away from the authorities in a Ford Explorer when he spotted them blocking off an intersection near his home. Mark Sellers had led a $10 million investment fraud scheme to fund his extravagant lifestyle, according to a federal court filing. Federal prosecutors in Kansas City unsealed a forfeiture request to seize Sellers' house, a 2014 Porsche 911, and five separate life insurance policies with a cumulative death benefit of $6 million, all of which investigators believe were ill-gotten gains from the fraud scheme. Mark Sellers killed himself that day. Authorities also believe that once Sellers spent all his investors' money, he turned to maxing out eight different credit cards in what is referred to as a "bust out" scheme. The moral to this story is eventually karma prevails. Could all of this have been prevented if Mark Sellers had been prosecuted by Macy's Board? It does prove that, eventually, crime does catch up with criminals and that the universe delivers justice, I believe that this is called karma.

Things for Macy's continued to get worse. R. H. Macy & Co., Inc. filed for Chapter 11 bankruptcy protection on January 27, 1992, after which point its banks fired the equity holder Ed Finklestein and his sons. After working on the LBO and working behind the scenes at Macy's for close to 7 years, this was the last thing that I would have ever expected. No white knight came in to save the day. Mike Ullman took over as CEO, and the B.O.B. became the EVP and CFO. Don Eugene stayed on in his role in California and became Secretary of the Corporation. This was a difficult time for the Company, those that had pledged their loyalty to Ed were publicly challenged, some were fired, others left on their own. There was great confusion and a lack of leadership. The preparation for the West coast conversion began in November and was slated for early May 1992. The epicenter for the systems conversion and migration was downtown Los Angeles at Hope & 8th

St. The Bullock's office facility was located north of South Central and east of Korea town and MacArthur Park in downtown Los Angeles. All through February, March & April, we prepared for the systems conversion. We trained staff in downtown Los Angeles on the new SABRE systems, and the staff in San Francisco were set up to handle the bankruptcy filing. The West EVP and the old Macy's California team handled the bankruptcy, and Don, me, and our team, handled the SABRE conversion.

The chaos and uncertainty of corporate America had taught me to expect the unexpected, but nothing could have prepared me for the storm brewing in Los Angeles. As the West Coast operations marched forward with the SABRE conversion and restructuring efforts, the tension in the air felt palpable, almost as if the city itself was warning of the turbulence to come. The shadows of mismanagement and greed still loomed large over Macy's, but the days ahead would test us not only in boardrooms and balance sheets but in the very streets where our stores stood. Little did I know, my time in Los Angeles would become less about corporate challenges and more about navigating a city engulfed in flames—both figuratively and, as I would soon witness, literally.

CHAPTER 6

Converting Systems in the middle of the LA Riots

On April 29, 1992, no one would have predicted what would happen. A jury acquitted three LAPD officers who had beaten Rodney King. Within hours of the acquittals, the 1992 Los Angeles riots began, lasting six days. African Americans were outraged by the verdicts and began rioting in the streets along with the Latino communities. By the time law enforcement, the California Army National Guard, the United States Army, and the United States Marine Corps restored order, the riots had resulted in 63 deaths, 2,383 injuries, more than 7,000 fires, damage to 3,100 businesses, and nearly $1 billion in financial losses. Smaller riots occurred in other U.S. cities such as San Francisco, Las Vegas in neighboring Nevada, Seattle in

Washington state, and as far east as Atlanta in Georgia and New York City.

On the night of the Rodney King verdict, I was having dinner in Santa Monica with Don and the SVP of Operations for I. Magnin. After dinner, I drove home to my hotel, the Westin Bonaventure, via the Harbor Freeway in downtown LA. As I drove over South Central, there were fires burning on either side of the highway, images like I remember seeing on the news as a kid of the Vietnam war. Flames, smoke, and chaos were everywhere. I was more than frightened, this wasn't like driving through downtown Newark, this was mayhem and dangerous. All exits off the freeway were blocked until I got downtown. As I pulled into the parking deck at my hotel and getting out of my car, I remember being screamed at by the attendant, "There is a curfew. Why are you driving on the street?"

Really, a curfew? I just drove through what seemed like hell, fires burning everywhere, I thought to myself. The next morning, I got up and walked to work. I saw many boarded-up buildings, storefronts, and gangs on street corners. The office at 8th and Hope was only 4 blocks from my hotel, and I walked very fast to the office. Only a skeleton staff had showed up to work that morning. I called Don Eugene; he was at Bullock's Wilshire office on Wilshire Blvd. He had just arrived from San Francisco; I left Bullocks and met him over at the Bullock's Wilshire building, now operated as I. Magnin. I remember sitting in his office, he was on the phone with the Los Angeles

Police Dept. (LAPD). They had called to tell us that an angry mob was approaching the store and that we should evacuate as soon as possible.

We jumped into the SVP of Operations car and drove to Newport Beach to escape the riot. On the way down on the freeway, we got a call from the security guards left in the I Magnin Bullock's Wilshire store. They had to abandon the building because the intruders had guns. That night, I slept in a hotel in Newport Beach and watched news coverage of people crawling out of the store windows of the Bullock's Wilshire store that I had just left. Looting was rampant all over Los Angeles. It was complete civil unrest that I had only heard stories of before in the late 60's but had never experienced first-hand. The next morning, SVP of Operations, Don and I returned to Bullock's Wilshire site on Wilshire Blvd. to meet insurance claims adjusters. As we were driving on Wilshire Blvd, there were gangs on the corner of MacArthur Park holding crow bars. I remember thinking to myself, I am going to die. We pulled up to the store, a historic building that had a Porte-cochere in the front and the back that had mosaic murals on the inside of the ceiling that were a favorite of Hollywood starlets and movie moguls. The store windows had all been smashed out. The store doors were gone. The cosmetic and jewelry cases on the inside of the store that were from the 1920s, 30s, and 40s were pulverized into tiny pieces of glass. Customer alterations were gone, display beds had been stolen, and most of the merchandise in the store was stolen. The dressing rooms that were at one time kept for special guests like John Wayne and Joan Crawford were destroyed. The store that was once referred to as the palace of commerce and elegance had been invaded and destroyed by looters. The upper floors were not damaged because fleeing staffers shut off the elevators; the original decision to build the store without escalators may have actually saved the landmark from ruin.

We made it up to the offices in the tower of the building, and Don called Mike Ullman to give him an update on the building and what was happening in Los Angeles. Mike was adamant that he did not want the SABRE conversion timetable to slip, even though we were in the middle of a riot and mandated curfew. Mike was new in his role and eager to impress the board. We pulled off the conversion without a hitch. Systems engineers were transported to 8th & Hope St. via Brinks Armored Trucks, and systems were converted and migrated to SABRE in Norcross, GA. Almost a week went by before any Macy's or I. Magnin store opened in the Los Angeles basin due to the curfews and civil unrest. It was surreal, as we stayed in a safe hotel in Beverly Hills and watched looting and tried to do work. The news was fixated on what was happening around us only 3 miles away. After this experience, I was not inclined to stay on the West Coast. I returned to my office in San Francisco and briefly started to look for a new job. I quickly realized all my business connections, friends, associates and my house were in NY and NJ. In fact, my house was still in mothballs per se. Although all my things had been placed in storage in a warehouse in South San

Francisco, I never sold my house, and I could just move back into Sleepy Hollow Lane in Plainfield. I spoke to Don and asked him if he could speak to Mike Ullman to see if there was a job I could take back in New York. There was, Mike needed someone to restart the Internal Audit Dept., and I was chosen to help do it.

The riots in Los Angeles left scars not just on the city but also on the people navigating the chaos, myself included. The eerie sight of a crumbling Bullock's Wilshire, once a beacon of elegance, haunted my thoughts as I returned to San Francisco to regroup. The West Coast had taken its toll, and while the SABRE conversion was a technical success, the emotional strain had left me yearning for the familiar rhythm of New York. When Don spoke to Mike Ullman about a potential role back East, the opportunity to rebuild Macy's Internal Audit felt like a lifeline. Little did I know, stepping back into the shuttered Bamberger's building in Newark would be less a homecoming and more a baptism by fire.

Chapter 7

Macy's Internal Audit

I returned to New York in July of 1992 to the shuttered Bamberger's building in downtown Newark. This is where Macy's Internal Audit Dept. was located, a building I had left 9 months earlier. I was quite familiar with the dept. The prior VP of Internal Audit was now working in Macy's East for the CFO Max Roberts. Don had nicknames for everyone. Don had nicknamed Max the Horrible Max with a wielding axe, who severed many a relationship already taxed. Max was asked to stay after the Sellers debacle. Max had previously run the Macy's Internal Audit dept. As an external auditor with Deloitte & Touche, I worked closely with Max. Years later, I met Max's son, who was working for Deloitte. He told me how he was afraid of Macy's Internal Audit growing up. He was afraid that they were going to arrest his father and take him away.

This was the furthest thing from the truth. There were four people in the internal audit dept, including myself. I was told the day I started that I had reported to a new group vice president who was responsible for internal audits but was not a certified public accountant or a certified internal auditor. The new GVP was a nice enough guy. The GVP dealt with Mike and The B.O.B. directly, and that was ok with me. The GVP did teach me about spreadsheets and data analytics, but he knew nothing about Macy's, the culture, the people, or where any of the bodies were buried, that is what I brought to the table. We seemed to tolerate one another, and he kept on telling me to save my money. I guess that meant my stay in the department would not be long. Given the fact that the Company was in the middle of bankruptcy, I was not sure any of us had much job security.

The GVP, Mike, and the B.O.B. put together an audit plan for the Dept. That is not the way Internal Aduit plans are supposed to be developed, but in this case, this is how it worked. I tried to explain to the GVP we had to focus on risk and, since we were in bankruptcy, where cash was being spent. I steered him towards construction and inventory since Macy's had outsourced Information Technology and had sold the credit card operations to General Electric. Those two risks were minimal now.

The B.O.B. liked the idea of Construction since she had issues with the creative people in store planning, and Mike liked the idea of inventory, particularly the foreign buying offices since that was Ed and his son Mitch's domain for decades, and no one ever was allowed to audit it. We started first by hiring some auditors, one of our best hires was Kathy Cushing, a former Controller of Gimbels. Next, we hired someone with expertise in construction, a former real estate construction controller. We hit the ground running and started with construction audits of new stores and major renovation projects. Right out of the gate, we found money being moved between projects, meaning if one project were under budget, they would move that money to cover a project that was over budget. Sounds right to me, huh? By the end of our first day, we found over $15 million in budget overruns hidden by transfers from project underruns. The entire project budget system needed an overhaul and there were no checks or balances in place to prevent this practice from reoccurring.

We then audited the Visual Dept. (at the request of management). The Visual Dept. was run by a seasoned veteran of the industry, Joe Cicio. The Office Manager was a gentleman from South Africa that was quite polite and very well dressed but did not know how to manage a budget, pay a bill, or do any accounting whatsoever. For whatever reason, he was put in charge of a $10 million annual visual display budget for the Herald Square store. The only problem was that the bills that were processed for this season were from last year. His explanation was that if he processed this season bills, he would be overbudget and get a beating from his manager, Mr. Cicio (according to Don, rumored to be a BDSM master). We did not ask any further questions as we had seen enough at this point.

To me, these audits were infantile, did not add any value, and were not worthy of my time, but Senior Management seemed to enjoy them. Internal Audit at Macy's was not by its charter an objective third line of defense nor independent. For the most part, people who were long-timers in the dept. were transferred there from another dept. because the Company could not get rid of them. This is sad because Internal Audit can be a valuable source of process improvement for a company and help to develop talent if the dept. is properly monitored, focused, and given the proper support and funding.

In December of 1992, the GVP and I met with the head of the Corporate Buying Office (CBO). The CBO GVP was new to his role. He had come from apparel manufacturing, a major supplier to the Limited. Macy's private Label program at this time accounted for almost 30% of merchandise sold in its stores and was a major source of profit. Unfortunately, controls over purchases from the CBO were weak or non-existent. The CBO GVP asked us to visit the Asian and the European offices and to perform audits. Macy's vast network of offices had been in existence in some areas since before World War I. Again, while the GVP understood merchandise and procurement, importing and loading, his duties as an auditor were foreign to him. I had spent years auditing the CBO while at Deloitte and had spent time working on a consulting project reconciling CBO and division accounting records, which was problematic. So, in early December of 1993, we departed for Hong Kong. This was my first trip to Hong

Kong. We had to leave in the middle of the night to land at the Hong Kong airport, in the time window we were allotted. The old Hong Kong airport had flight restrictions because of its location in the middle of Kowloon. Landing in Hong Kong was like parking a 747 in the middle of a very large apartment complex. I closed my eyes as we landed. Mitch Finklestein was still doing business with the office through his own company, WiseTex, and we met with Mitch, who seemed unscathed by the bankruptcy and the aftermath. Mitch was married to the daughter of Sir Run Run Shaw, an investor in LBO. He was a major supplier to many juniors' businesses in the US and in Asia. We found very few problems in Hong Kong, and this was a good opportunity to show and explain to the GVP how an office was supposed to work.

We spent a little over two weeks in Asia and returned to the US before the Holiday break. Once back at work after the New Year, the GVP wanted us to venture out into the European offices. We were delayed in our departure, the GVP to Madrid and Paris and me to Tel Aviv and Budapest, by the conflict in the Balkans. In late 1992 the US issued regulations that required all US Companies that were operating in Yugoslavia to cease operations. Macy's had an office in Belgrade and sourced outerwear from the surrounding regions, including Bulgaria and Albania. The office in Belgrade was moved north up the Danube to Budapest, Hungary. I left in early March 1994 first for Tel Aviv and then onto Budapest. The GVP started his European vacation at the same time. Both Madrid and Paris were small offices that had been in existence for more than 70 years and had seasoned employees. I had never traveled to Israel, and although briefed on the interrogation process before entering and leaving the country, I really did not know what to expect. I traveled on El Al out of JFK to Tel Aviv. I thought the questioning and the delay in boarding was extreme, as it took over an hour and a half. Once on the flight, I learned that the Israeli Prime Minister was on the same flight. I felt very safe.

March in Israel is still cold, not beach weather. I was shocked by the teenagers carrying assault rifles like kids carry backpacks here in the US. The offices in Tel Aviv for Macy's were modern, clean, and very well maintained. Macy's sourced cotton T-shirts and many of the same items that the GAP was sourcing at that time from the same vendors. I enjoyed the people and the food. I was not at ease because of the recent Arab scud missile bombings just north of the city. It was a dangerous place. Leaving Israel is just as difficult as arriving, the level of interrogation was high, and I kept on thinking to myself, what have I done? In hindsight, post 9-11, it was not me; it is just a necessary precaution to keep the aircraft safe.

The internal audit work was draining, not because of its complexity but due to the layers of dysfunction and mismanagement we uncovered at every turn. By early 1993, my trips to Hong Kong and Tel Aviv had shown me both the best and worst of Macy's operations overseas. But it was Budapest that would test my resolve in ways I had never imagined. As the plane descended onto the tarmac of a city still bearing the scars of Soviet occupation, I could sense that this was going to be no ordinary audit. What lay ahead would be a surreal mix of shadowy accounting practices, Cold War-era bureaucracy, and a glimpse into a city struggling to reinvent itself amidst chaos.

CHAPTER 8

Budapest

If you remember Hogan's Hero's on TV in the 70's, you can imagine what it was like to land in Budapest, Hungary, in mid-March of 1993. We landed on the tarmac, there was a very small airline terminal, more like an old bus station. As we departed down the stairs from the plane, we were greeted by men in dark green Army Uniforms goose-stepping and marching with German shepherds and rifles. Our luggage was brought out onto the tarmac in front of us, and we had to claim it there, there was no baggage claim area. The Berlin Wall fell in November of 1989, yet the last Soviet troops did not leave Hungary until almost two years later, and they demanded reparations for the investment they had made in Hungary. I arrived in Budapest 18 months after that, many described Budapest as a city like Paris after World War II and the German occupation.

Many US expatriates had returned to Hungary to reclaim their family property, like the family of Leonard and Estee Lauder, their son Ron had already built a restaurant and started making improvements to the Zoo. I made my way to a cab stand at the airport, the entire airport was gray, dungy, and smoke-filled. Many of the men still wore hats. It was like a bad Fellini film. I asked a cab driver to take me to the Grand Kempinski Hotel. It was a German chain that had just opened not far from the office. It was early in the afternoon when I arrived. There was a message for me when I arrived from the office: someone would meet me for dinner at 5:00 pm. I got cleaned up and was back in the Lobby at 5:00. I was greeted by a tall man over 6 ft tall who must have weighed over 250 lbs. He had a beard and wore round wire-framed glasses; his name was Igor, and he was the Managing Director of the Budapest Office.

That night Igor gave me a tour of Budapest, two cities, Buda and Pest. Buda, on the hill overlooking the Danube where the Citadel or Castle is at, was the home of the Former Prince of Austria-Hungary and Pest, the City with the wide boulevards modeled to be the Paris of Eastern Europe. The Danube was no longer blue but brown, and everything that you could imagine was wrong with Times Square, from Strip Clubs, Fast Food, and Cigarettes had populated the landscape. It was capitalism, Hungarian style, and Igor wanted to show off this magnificent city. He took me to the main casino, which was housed in the Citadel. It was a throwback to Rowan and Martin's Laugh-In, where women were dancing in cages in costumes from the 1960s. Everyone smoked, drank to excess, and played the roulette table. I just stood there in amazement, not knowing what to think, sure though not to offend Igor and to smile as the frolicking and carousing went on into the night. It must have been 3:00 am before I got back to my hotel.

The next day, a driver from the office picked me up and took me to Budapest's fanciest and most famous restaurant, Gundel. It was reopened in 1992 under the auspices of the well-known restaurateur Alan Lang, owner of New York's Café des Artistes. The Hungarian-born Lang, author of *The Cuisine of Hungary*, and his partner Ronald Lauder, son of Estée Lauder and a one-time New York gubernatorial candidate, spared no effort in attempting to re-create the original splendor for which Gundel, founded in 1894, achieved its international reputation."

I will tell you that this is not how an audit is performed. I thought to myself, what is happening here? I asked Igor after lunch if we could go to the office. He told me tomorrow there will be plenty of time to audit, today we enjoy Budapest. I went to bed early that night and, woke up early the next morning and found my own way to the office. It was only four blocks from the hotel. I was greeted by a nice Croatian woman named Maria. She was expecting me. She handed me piles of payroll records, invoices, petty cash receipts, and bank statements, all from the first day they had opened the office in Budapest. She told me that I would have lots of questions. That I did. I found receipts for cars, a Mercedes Benz 450 SL. I found receipts for guns AK47's. I found factory invoices from Belgrade and surrounding towns in the then Yugoslavia. Production of merchandise was being performed on Macy's behalf after the sanctions had been put in place. But the most creative thing that I saw were the payroll records. According to the CBO, there were 5 employees in the new Budapest office. I had payroll records for 26 employees. Who were these people? And how were they calculating the payroll? To my surprise, the employee's payroll was grossed up for their share and the Macy's share of the equivalent of Social Security and related payroll taxes.

It was still early in the morning; the office did not open until 10:00 am and it was 9:00. I made copies of all the pertinent records and returned to the Hotel. I sent a very long message to the General Counsel of R. H. Macy in Herald Square via the Fax machine. It was already after 5:00 pm in New York. I knew I would have to wait a day for the response. I went back to the office and Igor and his assistant Svetlana were waiting for me in Maria's office. They asked me if I had any questions. I told them I had only one question: how does the payroll calculation work? Igor explained that since none of the employees were Hungarian citizens, and that all of them wanted to continue their Yugoslavian benefits. Once a month, Svetlana would return to Belgrade and deposit the monies into everyone's account. Their Social Security Payments and payroll taxes as required. She did this once a month at the Central Bank, in Belgrade, I was told. I looked at Svetlana, who was looking at her feet, and at Igor, who smiled at me. I got up from the table and said, oh well, looks like the audit is over with, thank you so much for your help! There was no longer any Central Bank operating in Belgrade, and the former Yugoslavia was no longer in existence. Maria had just returned to the room and asked everyone if she could order lunch. I said I did not feel well and needed to return to the Hotel. This was the truth; I really did not feel well. I waited in my room in the Grand Kempinski for a day until I heard from the General Counsel's office. I received a telex. It was short and sweet and read, "Get out, return to Florence." Florence was the European headquarters for Macy's CBO.

Due to late winter storms in the Alps, it took another two days before I could get a flight out of Budapest. There were no direct flights to Florence, and I had to fly through Germany and change planes in Munich. By the time I got there, the new Managing Director of the CBO European Offices was there, and the internal audit GVP had arrived. He had finished his vacation in Madrid and Paris. We all flew to Budapest. We met others there and closed the entire office in the next few days. Igor left before we got back to Hungary. I am not sure what happened to him.

By the end of April 1993, I was back in my office in Newark, drafting a report on the European Office Audits. That report was never issued. By the end of May 1993, I was asked by the GVP to meet him in David Brown's office in Herald Square. David was the SVP of Human Resources. I was given a package that day. Six months' severance and six months' salary as a bonus for all my hard work. I had risked my life for Macy's in the LA Riots and in Budapest, and they were releasing me from my duties? The bottom line is that I knew too much. If the creditors' committee ever got hold of that report and found out the FCPA violations had occurred and were never reported, Mike, The B.O.B., and the Senior Management team would be out. Don called me from California that night at home. He said he did not know that I was being terminated. I suspect he did not know, as he was also on the chopping block. I saw my termination as retribution for Mark Sellers and how I testified against him. Mike Ullman was a vengeful man, and so was the B.O.B. They did not call her the B.O.B. for nothing.

I still remember that day I walked out of Macy's Herald Square for the last time, walking down my gravel driveway on Sleepy Hollow Lane. I was upset. I cried on the train ride home from Herald Square. I had done my best and was terminated, it was a cry that released a lot of pent-up anger and fear. I had an entire summer ahead of me, though, to garden and to heal from the trauma of Macy's. I was only 32 years old and had seen more and done more than most Senior Executives had in their entire careers.

Returning to Newark after the chaos in Budapest was like emerging from a storm only to find myself navigating uncharted waters. The termination package handed to me was both a relief and an insult, a quiet acknowledgment of my contributions and a stark reminder of how expendable even the most loyal could be. As I closed that chapter, I resolved to leave the politics and betrayals of Macy's behind, even as they lingered in my mind. But the world of retail had a way of pulling me back in, and by August, I found myself stepping into the hallowed halls of Bergdorf Goodman—a place where glamour reigned, the rules were different, and challenges of an entirely new kind awaited.

CHAPTER 9

The Easy Days at Bergdorf Goodman on the Plaza

By the beginning of August 1993, I had met with a lot of people about jobs in the city. One of my former clients from Deloitte was Bergdorf Goodman (BG), part of The Neiman Marcus Group (NMG), 60% owned by the Smith family of Harcourt General (General Cinema – Harcourt Brace Jovanovich). The former CFO had been recently promoted to President and Chief Operating Officer. The CEO was Burt Tansky, the longtime President of Saks Fifth Avenue. The CFO had worked his way up through the ranks at BG under Ira Neimark and Dawn Mello. Ira had recently retired after almost 18 years at the helm. Ira Neimark and Dawn Mello had turned BG into the foremost luxury retailer in the US and 2nd only to Harrods in fashion in the world. The CFO and Burt Tansky were now at the pinnacle of retailing at a store like no other.

The CFO needed help in the finance and systems area of the Company. Corporate in Boston wanted improvements to the bottom line. The CFO, now President, brought me in as a Vice President of Internal Audit, although my responsibilities were related to Inventory Control, Credit Fraud & Investigations, Expense Planning & Control, and special projects. I reported directly to the President. My office was next to the Fifth Ave Store manager, and we shared a secretary, Mona. Next to the store manager's office sat the President's cousin, SVP of Operations. The store manager was responsible for all selling and the Men's Store including merchandising. The SVP of Operations was responsible for Receiving, Supplies, Traffic, & Security. The President also had reporting to him the SVP of the Home Store, and the SVP and CFO (who the President referred to as Dumbsky), and the VP of Credit. Although Burt Tansky was the CEO, only the woman's store merchants, the visual team, and the Fashion Office reported to him. The head of the Fashion Office was Ellin Salzman. Ellin had worked at Saks with Burt but most recently for Ed Finklestein at Macy's. Dawn Mello was the previous President of BG and, with Ira Neimark, is credited for the success of Donna Karan, the five Fendi sisters, Michael Kors, Louis Dell Olio, and many other American fashion designers, including Tom Ford.

After the first month at BG, it seemed boring compared to what I had experienced at Macy's over the prior three years. While it was boring, the customers and the employees operated in a world where money was no object, an ostentatious show of wealth. On the slowest of days in the store, large sales were still recorded to celebrities, princesses, and uber-rich oligarchs, as Bergdorf was their place to shop and be seen on Fifth Avenue. The politics were enormous, from the salespeople to the buyers, the receiving dept. and even in the credit dept. Many of these people had worked together for almost 20 years. It was very cliquish, and no one wanted to change. Everything was done on old manual systems, and the President wanted change because Neiman's was growing rapidly with new stores and systems, and BG was not. I met with my boss once a week in a touch base meeting. The first area that we decided to attack was inventory shortage. At Macy's, this was a significant problem due to antiquated systems, outsourced receiving, multiple stores, and the sheer volume of transactions. BG, though only had two stores, the volume was high per square foot, but receiving was all in one place. The buyers were all in the same location. There were far fewer places that merchandise could be stolen. How could this Company be running the same shortage percentages as Macy's? Yes, it was a NYC store, and there was theft (remember Liza Minnelli stealing ties in the movie Arthur), but not these kinds of numbers.

We worked together with the buyers, store managers, security, visual, and operations and brought the inventory shortage down from over 3% to less than 1%. We attacked the areas with the highest and most inconsistent numbers, first, the home store and fine jewelry. What we found were bad inventory counts in the Home Store in counting of sets vs. eaches and theft. Yes, klepto-maniacs that lived on Park Ave. that were some of our best customers, helping themselves to silver and china. In the jewelry dept., we found that the buyers were holding jewelry in safes in their offices. The jewelry counts were never accurate, and items that had been missing for years on consignment were never properly accounted for. On the 4th floor, the couture dress dept. had a personal shopper that was famous with celebrities, the only problem was that merchandise would leave the store and was never returned and, in some cases, never charged to the customer. It was just being borrowed for a photo shoot, and we were getting publicity was a typical story. But the biggest issue of all was the missed markdowns. Instead of markdowns being taken on merchandise before it was sold, the merchandise was sold at the markdown price to the customer, but inventory was still on the books at the original price. How did this happen? The buyers and even the SVP of Woman's Merchandise were responsible for marking down the merchandise. Coming from a place like Macy's, I could not comprehend how buyers were responsible for marking down goods on the floor. Even in college at Stix, Baer & Fuller, salespeople were responsible for taking markdowns. Not at BG, the salespeople were some of the highest-paid people in the company. They were making 6% sales commission that translated in 1993 to over $125,000 a year. The most coveted position was selling shoes in the women's shoe dept. The average price of a woman's shoe was $2,000. Salespeople could not be asked to do menial labor like taking markdowns on the floor or even doing stockwork. BG had stock people; what were they doing?

Bergdorf Goodman was a world of contrasts—old-world opulence clashing with the inefficiencies of an outdated back office. While we managed to reduce shortages and streamline processes on the sales floor, it was clear that deeper changes were looming just below the surface. The politics of the store, the cliques among employees, and the precarious balance of independence from Neiman Marcus all painted a picture of an institution at a crossroads. As I began digging into the catalog and credit operations, the cracks in Bergdorf's facade became impossible to ignore. Change was inevitable, and the battle between tradition and progress was about to escalate.

CHAPTER 10

The merging of Bergdorf Goodman and Neiman Marcus back-office operations

My next project at BG, after we reduced shortage, got markdowns recorded in the right place, and improved gross margin dollars by giving the merchants a tool to go to their vendors to collect markdown allowances, was the Bergdorf Goodman Catalog. Bergdorf Goodman's catalog operation was all contained in the New York City Store and back offices. This included the production of the catalog, the photography, photo shoots, buying, mailing, data mining of mailing lists, and fulfillment. Yes, all catalog orders were filled from the selling floor. The merchandise in the catalog was in a separate dept., in some cases at a different price, but it was fulfilled from the same stock, from the sales floor. This is what the stock people were doing: filling catalog orders. The fulfillment rate on catalog orders was around 50%, that means that out of 100 orders, we were only able to fill 50 of them, or in other words, we were losing 50% of sales. The merchandise in the catalog was somewhat promotional and seasonal in nature. Some were private labels, and some were basic stock. The best-priced items and the basic stock items sold out first. As the buyers were not responsible for the Catalog, there was little or no incentive to build the business or to deal with backordered items. The Catalog Dept. tried to do everything and without systems, little got done.

The Neiman Marcus Group acquired the Horchow Collection in 1988 from Roger Horchow. They had just finished integrating their catalog operations into a shared facility in Grapevine, TX. The President asked me to go down to Neiman's with some others and look at it. The tour was noneventful. I had a client in public accounting, J. Crew and I knew catalog operations and accounting. J. Crew was one of the first large apparel catalog operators with a fulfillment operation, out of Lynchburg, VA. Not only could Nieman's-Horchow handle the Bergdorf Catalog's existing business, but they could also improve upon and grow it. This, though, was a delicate subject for the management of Bergdorf, they had watched others all around them disappear, Bonwit Teller, B. Altman, I. Magnin; would they be the next victim? Why couldn't they just change the name of Bergdorf Goodman to Neiman Marcus? The only branch store BG ever had in White

Plains was converted to Neiman's, why not the 5th Avenue store? You would surely save the cost of the back-office operations, receiving, credit, and advertising a separate brand? There was only one problem. Bergdorf Goodman and Neiman Marcus did not own the building at 754 Fifth Ave. The building belonged to the Goodman family. The Goodman family and its heirs first leased the store in 1972 to Carter Hawley Hale and then to its successor, Neiman Marcus Group. Andrew Goodman lived in the penthouse Apt. above the store until 1996. The lease required the name of the store to be operated in the space to be Bergdorf-Goodman.

Senior Management had staved off Neiman's overtures for years. They were highly profitable and were left to their own demise. If it is not broken, do not fix it was the attitude. The Men's Store, though, was open in 1990 to great fanfare, allowing more main store space to be used for women's apparel. The men's store, though by 1993, had not made its sales projections and was draining on the overall Company profitability. Burt Tansky had replaced Ira and was looking to expand his role with the parent company. Change was something that he wanted, and the President was not eager to accept it. Besides the Catalog operations, the question arose as to why BG needed a separate credit dept. I was asked to look at this and give my opinion. I was told that the BG customer was different than the NM customer. Growing up in St. Louis, I shopped at NM at Plaza Frontenac when there was a sale. Moving to New York, I could use my NM credit card at BG. In fact, BG customers could use their BG cards at any NM store. I asked to see an analysis of the crossover of customers. What was evident was that NY customers visited or vacationed in markets where there was an NM shop there. BG customers shopped in Beverly Hills, San Francisco, Scottsdale, Bal Harbor, and Chicago, and NM customers from all over the US shopped at BG in New York.

The VP of Credit gave me an example why they needed to be separate, celebrities like Sammy Davis Jr. only paid their bill once a year. The BG credit dept. knew how to take care of these kinds of customers and not put them in collection. I visited the NM Credit dept., in fact, they had the exact same situation, only they had many more celebrities shopping in their stores than BG as they had many more stores. It seemed that the feedback was just not holding water for BG. The credit dept. occupied a floor in a separate bldg. adjacent to the store on 57th street. This was a four-story bldg. The advertising, marketing, and catalog dept. had the 2nd floor, the Accounting, Sales Audit, Import and Accounts Payable Dept. was on the 3rd floor and the credit dept. was on the 4th floor. The rent for this bldg. at 5th Ave and 57th St was $100 per sq. ft. The rent in Grapevine Tx at the new Nieman's-Horchow facility was $4 per sq. ft. To me it seemed obvious what was about to happen, I lived through this same phenomenon for 3 years at Macy's. Cost savings and job reductions were happening, it was just a matter of time.

As the consolidation of Bergdorf Goodman's back-office operations unfolded, the inevitable friction of change began to surface. The elegant facade of Fifth Avenue hid the harsh realities of cost-cutting and efficiency mandates, and the old guard clung tightly to their ways. But just as the dust began to settle, a call from Harcourt General would set me on an entirely different path—one that would test my judgment, my loyalty, and my ability to navigate the tangled web of corporate politics. It was time to look beyond the balance sheets and dive into the murky waters of internal accountability.

CHAPTER 11

Investigating the Boss

About this time, I received a call from the Controller of Harcourt General. It seemed that there was an alleged kick-back scheme in the supply area of BG. It had been reported by the Director of Procurement of Neiman Marcus in Dallas, TX. I informed the Controller that I needed to run this by the President. He informed me that he had spoken to Burt Tansky, and since the supply dept. reported to the SVP of Operations, the President's cousin, neither could be involved in the investigation and that I needed to hire whoever could assist me and report back to him and Burt Tansky the results. I had never been asked to investigate my boss or his cousin before. While the President openly called the SVP of Operations an idiot in meetings and referred to him as a buffoon, the President had hired SVP of Operations 17 years earlier and promoted him to his current position, and the SVP of Operations was one of his men. The President was the kind of boss you would not cross. He was extremely bright and insightful, but I had also started to see a different side of him, one of vindictiveness and intimidation, although not quite as extreme as the Sphinx. As I started to inquire about the supply area, I talked to many people in the industry and ended up hiring one of my former employee from Macy's, Kathy Cushing. She was the first woman Controller of a major retailer, the great Gimbels of Philadelphia. She had gone on to be a CFO in the world of apparel for Vera Wang, amongst others, and was doing consulting. Federated had taken over Macy's and all the Finance and Accounting jobs in New York and Newark were relocated to Cincinnati less than 12 months after I had left Macy's. She, too, had great instincts and knew retailing like the back of her hand. Given the situation I was now in, she was a person I needed to help me. We both called the procurement dept. at Neiman Marcus in Dallas to find out what the specific allegations were. They were not detailed, just that we were overpaying for bags and boxes. We asked how did they know this? The answer was BG would not bid out their supplies with Neiman's orders to save money. We scratched our heads and asked why? It seemed that BG used a middleman to procure bags, boxes, and supplies for a Company in Long Island City. This Company also had a warehouse that operations used to store supplies, fixtures, and visual used it, as well as their staging facility.

These allegations happened in January, and I started working on the investigation after the inventory had been reconciled. I remembered from working on the 7th floor during Christmas that we kept running out of bags and boxes. Bags and boxes are packed in boxes of 500, no one ever opens the carton of boxes and counts the number of bags to make sure that we got 500 bags or boxes and that we were not shorted. Based on the number of point-of-sale transactions during the Holiday selling period, it seemed that we were running a 20% shortage of bags and boxes. We pulled the invoicing from the vendor and the purchase orders, and it said the vendor had reduced the price to meet the price offered by the Neiman Marcus Group bid. So, if the vendor lowered the price by 10% to meet a Corp. price and shorted the number of bags and boxes by 20%, they in fact, increased the per unit price by 12.5%. This would have been why we were running out of bags and boxes. Now, all we had to do was prove it.

We walked downstairs to the basement of the main store on Fifth Ave. to meet with the Purchasing Manager. The purchasing manager had been hired by the President and now worked for The SVP of Operations. We asked the purchasing manager where they stocked bags and boxes. We found several unopened cartons of bags in all the various sizes. The largest bag came in quantities of 250. We asked them to open the box and count the number of bags, he looked at us like we were crazy. He opened the box and counted 199 bags. We found another unopened carton of large bags, and there were only 201 bags. We asked the purchasing manager if we should open another box, he quickly said no. We had an invoice for a shipment of large bags with us, and it indicated that 250 large bags were contained in each box. We also showed him the purchase order that said the same thing. He just shook his head in disbelief. He had no explanation; he did not know what to say. Kathy and I left his office in the basement and returned to my office and called the Director of Procurement at Neiman Marcus. We asked him if they could explain to us how their bags were shipped and packed. He asked us if we had found that the bag count was shorted? How did he know this? We asked him, on point, why would he think this. He told us that a year ago, when he started in this job at Neiman's, they were having significant bag count shortages. He also said that based on his experience in this role with other retailers, this type of shorting and overbilling practice was very common. He was suspicious that the same thing was happening at BG when they refused to switch vendors. NM had instituted spot checks and field audit techniques to spot this practice, and they had significant expense savings. He also had to let go several old-timers in his dept.

At this point, we proved that we had a dishonest vendor. We did not prove that we had dishonest employees. I met again with the purchasing manager and, this time, with the Head of Store Security. I let the Store Security Director question him. He blamed the vendor and blamed the SVP of Operations, and the President for bullying and mistreating him for years. The purchasing manager would not explain but admitted to knowing that the vendor was overbilling the Company. He did not explain how he knew. He got up from his desk and left. After almost twenty years, he just walked out of the building, gave us his employee ID, and said he was tired of being bullied, blamed, and intimidated. The purchasing manager took the wrap. It all seemed too easy, almost planned. I reported back to the Corp. Controller and Burt Tansky the results. Kathy wrote a report, and we started a major process to clean-up the supplies operation and accounting. Neiman Marcus took over all supply procurement and storage in their NJ warehouse. The SVP of Operations and the Director of Visual were sent to Long Island City to clean out the warehouse where supplies and visual props were stored. In my weekly meetings with the President, I heard nothing else about the supplies adventure. One night, as I exited the 57th Street door, Mr. Tansky walked out at the same time. He told me I did a good job cleaning up the supply mess. That was it; it was now the end of April 1994, and I had been at BG for less than 1 year.

In Spring of 1994, rumors began to swirl that Burt Tansky was to be promoted to CEO of Neiman Marcus in Dallas and that the President would be the new CEO of BG. It was also at this time that they announced the return of Dawn Mello to her prior role as President of BG. She returned with great fanfare, but not before Ms. Mello and the CEO fired Ellin Saltzman. The firing of Ellin Saltzman played out of the front page of Woman's Wear Daily like an assassination. Ellin and Ms. Mello were archrivals in the fashion world for decades, Ellin at Saks and Dawn at BG. Ellin never seemed to realize that she was no match for Dawn Mello. Dawn discovered Donna Karan, Michael Kors, Tom Ford and made them all famous, and held her ground against the great Geraldine Stutz at Henri Bendel for over a decade. Ms. Mello dressed Princess Dianna, Michael Jackson, and every A-lister there was in the 90's. The return of Dawn Mello to BG was indeed a major coup for the store.

I was promoted to VP, Controller, and Chief Accounting Officer in May of 1994. I also was given stock options in NMG. I still reported to the CEO. Things really did not change that much, at least from the outside. By the fall of 1995, Neiman Marcus opened its 2nd store in NJ at the Mall at Short Hills. They already had a store in King of Prussia, Pa, and one in Paramus, NJ. Their distribution center was in Secaucus. Our first meeting with NM management was in the Short Hills store in the late Summer of 1995, prior to its opening. We met with the head of Information Technology and Neiman Marcus's CFO. He had been the CFO of Bullock's prior to the acquisition of Macy's. When Alan Questrom and Terry Lungren (prior CEOs of Neiman Marcus) arrived at Neiman's from Bullock's, they hired the former Bullock's CFO. He was instrumental in implementing new systems at Neiman's. Systems were BG's downfall and weak point, just like Macy's, and left them vulnerable. The CEO had put Dumbsky in charge of systems, and this was probably one of his biggest mistakes.

After the meeting in Short Hills, I knew the writing was on the wall. The catalog and credit operations had moved or were transitioning to Dallas. The other two floors in the building on 57th St. contained the Accounting Dept. and Advertising. Advertising reported to Ms. Mello. The CEO fired the SVP of Advertising that Spring. When he left, he sent a very strange email to all his contacts, including the CEO. He mentioned how much he enjoyed working at BG as it was a job that he would remember for the rest of his life. He also said, unlike the rumors about the CEO, he did not threaten, torture or bully him into leaving the Company. I thought it was quite strange as it was clear that the SVP of Advertising was terminated.

With the supply investigation closed and a fresh wave of changes sweeping through Bergdorf Goodman, I couldn't shake the sense that the ground beneath us was shifting faster than anyone wanted to admit. The arrival of new leadership only added to the unease, as back-office transitions gained momentum and longstanding traditions began to crumble. Just as I thought I had a handle on the chaos, the CEO introduced a fresh challenge—one that would test not just my expertise, but my integrity. It was clear that the next chapter would be anything but predictable.

CHAPTER 12

Cooking the Books

My first budget was due to Corporate for the Spring Season (beginning in February 1995) by November 1st, just after we had closed the 3rd qtr. It seemed very odd that we needed to recast the entire budget since we had a July 31st year-end, but that is what Harcourt General wanted. The CEO was fixated on the headcounts by dept. I remember taking the headcounts from payroll and, putting them on a schedule and watching the CEO reduce them by 20%. I did not follow how he was going to do that. It was November 1st, and we had no projects underway to reduce headcounts. He then told me to increase the foreign office load for the payroll that we were eliminating in the plan. While I was very familiar with this sort of accounting. It was wrong. Retail accounting of this nature artificially inflates the cost of inventory. In essence, you are capitalizing expenses into inventory. While the inventory load can be eliminated, expense transfers from the general ledger to the retail stock ledger are fraudulent and irregular accounting. I would not record these types of entries, and I did not instruct others to do so. To show an aggressive plan to Corporate is one thing, but to cook the books is something I have never done and would never do as a CPA. I cautioned the CEO that if we gave Corporate an aggressive plan, what would happen if we did not make it? He had no response. Also, Corporate did not want to receive the plan from Dumbsky, which I thought was strange. Instead, they wanted it from me.

I hired a former audit manager from Deloitte and from Macy's to help me reduce costs and improve controls in my area. She was someone that the CEO liked, although she was weary of him from the beginning. She was outspoken, very smart and, helped me reduce headcounts, and was excellent in process improvements. She was quick-witted, personable, and sometimes too smart for her own good. After we submitted the budgets, Christmas was upon us, and concentrating on making business happen in the store was the priority, in addition to finding more ways to reduce headcounts. We made a lot of progress, but I was kept in the dark about how fast and aggressive Neiman's was trying to absorb BG, especially now that Tansky was at the helm and had a mandate from Corporate. Christmas at the corner of Fifth Ave and 57th St is like magic in New York. The decorations and Holiday displays were amazing, especially at Bergdorf's. A fresh evergreen wreath on every window with a simple red bow is how the building was packaged, looking up from the sidewalk. I tried the same thing on my house on Sleepy Hollow Lane in Plainfield, but it just was not the same. The store visual dept. would work for weeks on the interior window displays, and they were the most intricate and exquisite. Dawn Mello hired Linda Fargo, who had left I. Magnin, where she had been groomed by the great Joe Cicio, she did things to the windows that to this day draw crowds to from across the world.

In early Spring 1996, the CEO met with all his direct reports and introduced us to a new EVP of BG. He was there to help the CEO manage. What they did not say though, was to help manage through the transition of the remainder of the back-office operations from New York to Dallas. My assistant Controller was very nervous and outspoken. She wore the emotions of every buyer, sales manager, and executive on her sleeve. She was rightly so; she was tired of leaving one retailer for another that was going through transition and downsizing. I also was getting quite anxious, even after all I had gone through at Macy's did I need to find a job yet again?

One of the first things that EVP asked me to do was to take over the new Point of Sale system conversion. We were converting to Neiman's system. Since I had experience doing conversions at Macy's this should be a breeze to me. I had been in my new job for about 18 months as Controller. How would I pull this off? I mentioned this to my Assistant, and she went ballistic. Her point was, why am I doing Dumbsky's job? Dumbsky was the CFO, yet I had taken over his responsibilities for accounting, and all he had left was Information Technology (IT). Why doesn't he do it? In hindsight, she was overwhelmed by the fact that she would have had to take over more of my responsibilities if I was working on this IT conversion. I told the EVP no this was not my responsibility. This was the first time I have ever told a boss no. I really was out on a limb here. The CEO came to see me and told me to go visit the Foreign Offices in Europe for BG and Neiman's as no one had been there in years. He knew I had experience in this area. He said, take some time to yourself and come back refreshed.

As I boarded the flight to Europe, I hoped this trip would offer not only a change of scenery but also some clarity. Little did I know that the moments of peace I found strolling through Parisian streets and meeting with office managers would be fleeting. The challenges awaiting me back in New York would make the past seem almost trivial in comparison. With every cab ride and conversation overseas, I was inching closer to a storm brewing back home—one that would threaten not only my career but my very integrity.

CHAPTER 13

Retribution for Telling the truth

I planned a trip to all the NMG buying offices. NMG operated offices in London, Paris, Milan, Florence, and we had vendors to meet with in Rome. It was a two-week trip. I first landed in Paris. The first night I was in Paris, I walked the city all night long. It was May, the weather was beautiful. The Office Managers treated me like royalty. It was professional royalty, not like in Hungary. I visited vendors, freight forwarders, and the offices. I spent time in Milan, Florence, London, and lastly in Rome. I had spent more than a week before in Florence while dealing with the Hungarian debacle, so I was very familiar with all the places in Florence as it is a small and compact city. Rome, though, is a whole other story. I needed to visit an Italian factor, one that factored receivables for the Fendi's. It was on the outskirts of the city. It took me four cabs before

I found I cab that would take me to the office address I needed to go to. You see, in Rome, it is not unusual for a cab driver to tell you to get out of their cab if they do not want to take you to your desired destination. I should have listened to cabbies in Rome that told me to "get out" of their cabs, but instead gotten out of Bergdorf Goodman. What the CEO had done so often to other people was about to happen to me.

As soon as I returned, the proverbial shit hit the fan. I was summoned into the EVP's office with the new VP of Human Resources. The HR VP explained to me that the Company had observed me in the Men's room on the seventh floor having sex with another man and that was a violation of store policy and that I could be dismissed. I laughed at both of them, telling them that they were mistaken. The CEO then entered the room and spoke to me privately, he told me that if I agreed to cooperate with him and the Company, all charges would be dropped, and I would be eligible for a special bonus package and off-the-books profit sharing. I was flabbergasted. I was being blackmailed. What the purchasing manager, the SVP of Advertising, and many others had said now made sense to me, the CEO and his associates at Bergdorf Goodman were like the Jewish mafia, and I was just expected to do what they asked or be ruined. I was stunned, the CEO told me to take the rest of the day off and think about it. This time, I was adamant that these fraudsters were not going to get away with this.

I walked down Fifth Ave and into the office of Ed Finklestein and Don Eugene. Don and Ed were working together in a consulting practice. I told both of them the entire story. Ed said this is what they did to people in 1960. You cannot let them get away with it. I then met privately with Don, and he gave me the name of a labor attorney. This happened in June 1996, almost three years to the day after I had left Macy's. I was very upset and again cried on the train home to Plainfield. This was going to be a long summer. I contacted Don's attorney and met with him and told him the entire story. I had to pay him a retainer, and according to the Code of Conduct and Ethics I had signed when I received my stock options, I was required to report everything to Harcourt General in Boston. My attorney contacted them immediately. I wrote down everything I knew about at BG, the investigation I was asked to do of the CEO, SVP of Operations and supplies, the manipulation of the budgets, and the headcounts. I also gave them copies of SVP of Advertisings email and details of the conversation with the purchasing manager. The legal dept. agreed to meet with me in Boston the following week. I had been suspended from my position at BG pending the results of an investigation. The outside accountants from Deloitte were engaged to ascertain if any accounting irregularities had occurred. I met with the legal dept. with my attorney, and they listened. Deloitte performed their review and spoke to many people and did not find any irregular accounting or improprieties; of course, they did not, I would not have permitted it. This process took until the end of August

1996. One week later, by Federal Express, right after Labor Day, I received a letter at my home informing me that I was terminated, as management had lost confidence in my abilities. They had lost confidence in my abilities to cook the books. New York is a right-to-work state, and everyone is an at-will employee. I was devastated. Friends in the industry called me and said they had heard someone in Finance at BG was caught having sex in the men's room at BG and was fired. They had smeared my good name, and I was deeply depressed, this was not true.

As a gay man, I marched up Fifth Ave with ACT UP to support those with AIDS in the late 80's. I had watched friends from college die of the deadly disease, only to be spared myself. I was in a committed relationship with a long-term partner at this point and really did not know who to turn to. I called Don Eugene and told him what happened. He told me that I could not give up, I needed to fight. Ed Finklestein weighed in. Ellin Salzman had worked for him at Macy's before the bankruptcy, and NMG and the CEO had also treated her poorly. They both encouraged me to keep fighting. They referred me to another attorney, one who would take my case on a contingency basis, and he was the fighter that I needed. He filed a lawsuit against Neiman Marcus Group for wrongful termination and discrimination based on Sexual Orientation. After all the bad press in WWD from the termination of Ellin Salzman, NMG did not want this across the front page to tarnish the good name of Bergdorf Goodman. The demand letter was sent to NMG in Boston in October. They requested that we wait for an answer for 30 days. We waited. After 30 days passed, there was still no response. My new attorney assured me that good news was coming but that I needed to be patient. By Thanksgiving, I signed a release of my claim, and they paid me one year's salary.

In March of 1999 (a year and a half after I made my settlement with NMG), across the front page of Woman's Wear Daily, it was announced that the CEO had resigned. as did the EVP, Dumbsky, SVP of IT, and SVP of Operations. All the back-office operations in New York had already been moved to Dallas and a major remodel of the NY store was announced to be overseen by Ms. Mello. The receiving facility in the basement was moved to Neiman's facility in Secaucus and remodeled into a new cosmetic dept. along with a renovation of the main floor. The CEO and his associates had worked together for over 20 years. They watched almost every major dept. store and specialty retailer in the US be downsized or disappear. They lasted so long because of the location their store, Fifth Ave. and 57th St., across from the Plaza Hotel and Central Park, once the home to Cornelius Vanderbilt's mansion.

Yes, I did feel some level of vindication. I still would rather have been treated fairly, to begin with. I was an adult, if they did not want me or need me, they should have discussed it with me, and we could have come to an amicable agreement. Unfortunately, in business, politics get involved, and egos get in the way. I was forever grateful though to Ed and Don for their help and moral support. They were honorable men. Karma and the universe had spoken.

CHAPTER 14

Moral of the Story – The Buried Truths of Corporate America

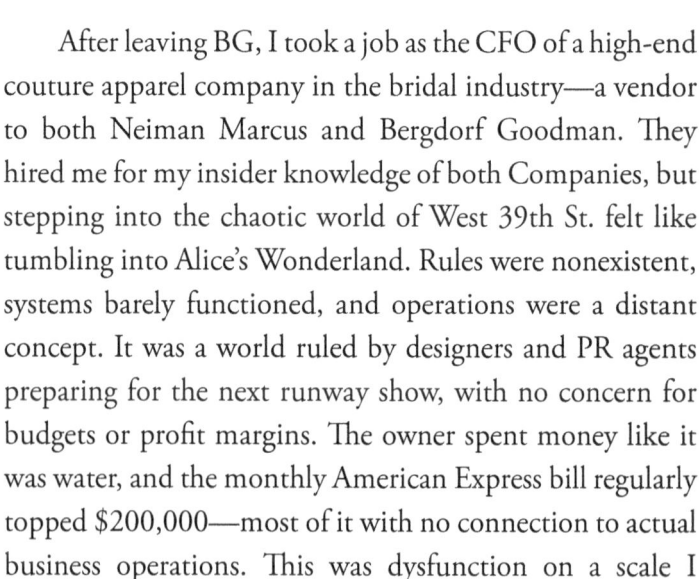

After leaving BG, I took a job as the CFO of a high-end couture apparel company in the bridal industry—a vendor to both Neiman Marcus and Bergdorf Goodman. They hired me for my insider knowledge of both Companies, but stepping into the chaotic world of West 39th St. felt like tumbling into Alice's Wonderland. Rules were nonexistent, systems barely functioned, and operations were a distant concept. It was a world ruled by designers and PR agents preparing for the next runway show, with no concern for budgets or profit margins. The owner spent money like it was water, and the monthly American Express bill regularly topped $200,000—most of it with no connection to actual business operations. This was dysfunction on a scale I hadn't yet encountered, and it left me questioning whether accountability had any place in luxury retail.

One of the first employees I had to deal with was the VP of Product Development—a character straight out of a satire about Madison Avenue excess. Her job was to scour the luxury boutiques on Madison for designs to knock off, racking up $20,000 in expenses without so much as a receipt. When I asked her for documentation, she looked at me with disdain and said, in her haughty Philadelphia lockjaw voice, "On whose authority am I to ask her for receipts?" I couldn't help myself: "Have you ever heard of the Internal Revenue Service?" She stared at me, stunned, as though I'd just introduced a foreign concept.

But that absurd encounter was only the warm-up act. The following week, I found myself in the office of the designer's father, where a leather suitcase sat conspicuously on his desk, stuffed with over $100,000 in cash. He calmly informed me that my job as CFO included delivering this suitcase to the head of the Ladies' Garment Workers Union to avoid paying union dues. I stared at him in disbelief. "You're asking me to bribe the union representative?" I said, incredulous. He didn't flinch. "Yes. That's how things are done." It was a moment of clarity—I knew then and there this was a line I wouldn't cross. I then was escorted out the office.

Upon return to my office on West 39th St. the next day, I was told that I had made the designer's father very angry. They told me that it was my last day, asked me to sign a non-disclosure agreement, and they paid me 6 months' severance. I told the designer, thank you! I was truly relieved as I was not willing to participate in a bribery scheme with the Union. Unfortunately, over the next 25 years, this was not the last pay-off that I received for refusing to participate in a fraud scheme or for reporting fraud and nefarious acts.

After the corporate failures of Enron and WorldCom, the world of corporate governance, accounting, and internal controls changed. In 2002, Congress enacted the Sarbanes-Oxley Act (SOX), that required internal controls to be put in place and a framework for measuring compliance, this is the law. While SOX has been a windfall for the accounting industry, it has one major flaw: who or what measures the truth? Internal controls are not about adding numbers together. They are about the structure, governance, risk assessments, and controls and monitoring of them. Management is charged with monitoring its own controls. This assumes that management is competent and objective.

There are several practical questions that make the monitoring of the internal controls function difficult to ascertain. What happens in a public company when fraud is reported? If the fraud involves Senior Management, it is supposed to be investigated by the Board of Directors, including the Audit Committee. The Board of Directors are then to be advised as to how management has dealt with the problem. What are the safeguards to ensure that this happens? What happens to the whistleblower or employee that brings the crime to the attention of the Company? What happens to them when they report their truth, and no one wants to hear it or act upon it. Are whistleblowers always fired? In my experience, most or either let go or demoted to positions that do not utilize their talents.

NYSE companies are required to have at least one financial expert on every audit committee. The rules also require an internal audit function. Can internal audit really be independent if they report to the Chief Financial Officer (CFO), who gives them a raise or gives them a performance review? What happens if the internal auditor finds his boss cheating? I once reported to a CFO, who never gave me a performance review and never communicated to me my annual raise. I would just have to wait until I got my pay stub to see my raise. The message that this sent was clear. I do not value your job, and I do not care if you stay or leave the Company. The tone at the top is what defines how corporate governance and rules operate and whether they are taken seriously. In the previous case, outwardly the CFO and the Company's actions spoke to their lack of interest in maintaining a competent Internal Audit function. How was the CFO allowed to conduct himself in this manner? The answer is simple, the Internal Audit function was not seen as a viable or contributing dept. but was only there as a requirement of the NYSE rules.

I was only 32 years old when I was let go from my job as a Vice President Internal Audit R. H. Macy & Co. Inc. with a package. This was the first time I was paid off to leave a Company for doing the right thing. I reflected on my life and what was important to me at this time after all that I had been through. I reflected on all the people that had lost their jobs because of Macy's bankruptcy and all the other department store bankruptcies that preceded Macy's and followed. An entire industry was decimated because of greed. Corporate raiders, investment bankers, and others destroyed Federated Department Stores, Allied Stores, Associated Dry Goods, and now Macy's. Locally owned or managed department stores would be a thing of the past. This was the evolution of retail. Big box stores like Walmart, Target, and BestBuy, and the internet, post COVID, have taken the place of local department stores. Merchandise at either end of the spectrum, high-end or low-end, is thriving. The department stores serving the middle class shrunk. In the early 90's the middle class began to falter, and two income earners were needed to support their families. Was Reaganomics to blame, or was it offshoring of jobs and manufacturing of goods and services to blame?

Is there a moral to the story? Does all fraud and corruption get reported, investigated, and remediated? How about the effect on the whistleblower?

Firing or laying off, demoting, denying overtime or promotion, disciplining, denying benefits, failure to hire or rehire, intimidation, harassment, and making threats are all real and frequent occurrences that whistleblowers endure. Most times, the person that becomes the whistleblower is doing the job that is required of them, including reporting that is required by a Company's code of conduct and ethics. Why would anyone want to do what is the right thing if they are terminated for doing what is required of them? How can investors make sure that they are investing in a Company that is not riddled with nefarious characters? Are profits and earnings the only thing that matters? How good are the reported earnings if shenanigans and cooking of the books go undetected?

Overly dominant CEO's that inflict pain on others and demand that subordinates follow their narcissistic orders are an enormous risk to an organization or to the company. In the case of Macy's, Mark Sellers went on to continue to commit more crimes and injure others and ultimately took his own life. As for the CEO of Bergdorf Goodman, how was his menacing behavior tolerated for so many years before any action was taken? Would either one of these retail leaders have been terminated for their reigns of terror on employees without the brave acts of whistleblowers? In these two situations, I believe that it was a lack of Board leadership, nepotism coupled with an unbridled fear of what would happen to the Company if the public ever found out what was really happening inside the walls of these esteemed and fabled organizations. I believe this is what is referred to as being swept under the proverbial carpet.

In the end, I've come to realize that integrity has its price—a price I've paid time and time again. I've seen firsthand how greed, unchecked power, and a relentless fear of exposure can rot even the most celebrated organizations from within. But I've also witnessed the power of standing up, even when the odds are stacked against you. My journey has been a long one, filled with betrayals and hard lessons, but through it all, I've held on to the belief that doing the right thing matters, even when the rewards are hard to see.

The truth is, change doesn't happen overnight. Justice isn't perfect. But every time someone speaks up, it chips away at the walls of corruption and fear that so many people hide behind. Maybe I didn't win every battle, but I can live with the decisions I've made. And in a world that often rewards silence, I'm proud to say that I chose to speak the truth—even when it cost me everything. That, I believe, is a legacy worth leaving.

Glossary

Arthur Andersen & Co.
One of the eight largest accounting firms that collapsed after the Enron fiasco.

Associated Dry Goods
A conglomerate that owned retailers across the U.S., including Lord & Taylor, JW Robinson, Stix Baer & Fuller, and Caldor. Acquired by the May Department Stores Company.

Allied Stores Corp.
A conglomerate that owned Ann Taylor, Jordan Marsh, Stern's, and many other stores. It was acquired by Campeau Corp. in a hostile takeover in the mid-1980s.

Bamberger's
A New Jersey-based department store founded by Louis Bamberger. It was later acquired by R.H. Macy & Co., Inc.

Campeau Corp.

A Canadian real estate company founded by Robert Campeau that acquired Allied Stores and Federated Department Stores in leveraged buyouts.

Crazy Eddie

A chain of electronics stores in the New York metro area, founded by Eddie Antar. The company was investigated by the Securities Exchange Commission for shareholder fraud and embezzlement.

General Dynamics

A large government contractor known for building nuclear submarines, among other things.

Loews Corp.

A conglomerate founded by Bob and Larry Tisch. It owned CNA Financial, Lorillard Tobacco, Bulova Watch, Loews Hotels, and several oil & gas companies.

May Department Stores Company

A large retail operation headquartered in St. Louis, MO, that owned Payless Shoes, Build-A-Bear, Venture, and department stores across the U.S., including Hecht Co. and May Company California. They acquired Marshall Field's and were, in turn, acquired by Federated Department Stores after its acquisition of R.H. Macy & Co., Inc.

NMG (Neiman Marcus Group)

Owner of Neiman Marcus, Bergdorf Goodman, and Casual Corner. The group was 60% owned by Harcourt General (Harcourt Brace Jovanovich and General Cinema).

Sarbanes-Oxley Act (SOX)

Legislation enacted by Congress in 2002 requiring certification of internal controls for publicly held companies.

R.H. Macy & Co., Inc.

The Macy's department store chain, which included subsidiaries such as Macy's New York, Bamberger's, Macy's California, Macy's Corporate Buying Offices, Bullock's, Bullock's Wilshire, I. Magnin, and Macy's South.

SEC (Securities & Exchange Commission)

A federal agency responsible for monitoring the stock market and public filings made by companies.

Touche Ross

One of the eight largest accounting firms. Later became Deloitte & Touche. It served as the external auditor for R.H. Macy & Co., Inc. and Loews Corporation.

Bullock's

A prestigious department store chain based in California, later merged with Macy's West.

SABRE Conversion

A systems integration project at Macy's involving new technology for inventory and operations management.

La Habra Store

A Macy's facility in Los Angeles County involved in inventory discrepancies and fraud investigations.

Budapest Office

A European outpost of Macy's Corporate Buying Office that highlighted fraud and mismanagement during audits.

People

Donald Eugene
Secretary and Controller of R.H. Macy & Co., Inc., a mentor and trusted guide.

Dr. Henry Kissinger
Head of the U.S. State Department, diplomat, and Audit Committee Member of Macy's.

Mark S. Sellers
Former Controller of Bullock's, Sanger-Harris, and Stix Baer & Fuller. Later became EVP of Macy's East.

Jerry Loeb
CFO of the May Department Stores Company.

David Farrell
CEO of the May Department Stores Company, often nicknamed "Darth Vader."

B.O.B.
CFO of Macy's during bankruptcy. Nicknamed "Beast of Belson" or "Bitch of Buchenwald" by Donald Eugene.

Larry Tisch
Chairman and co-founder of Loews Corp. and member of the R.H. Macy & Co. Board of Directors.

Ira Millstein
Lead partner at Weil, Gotshal & Manges and member of Macy's Board of Directors. Nicknamed "Cardinal Richelieu."

Ed Finkelstein
Chairman of R.H. Macy & Co., Inc.

Daniel Finkelstein
Chairman of Macy's California and Macy's West.

Mitch Finkelstein
Managing Director of Macy's Corporate Buying Office in Hong Kong.

Myron Ullman III ("Mike")
CEO of R.H. Macy & Co., Inc. Nicknamed "the small mouth."

Matty the Horse
Reputed mobster Matthew Ianniello.

Ron Perelman
Chairman of Revlon.

Rose Mario Bravo

Divisional Merchandise Manager of Cosmetics at Macy's. Later rebranded Burberry of London as Chairwoman.

Bob Chavez

Cosmetics buyer at Macy's and later the U.S. Head of Hermès.

Burt Tansky

CEO of Bergdorf Goodman and Neiman Marcus. Former President of Saks Fifth Avenue.

Ira Neimark

Former Chairman and credited founder of the modern Bergdorf Goodman.

Dawn Mello

President of Bergdorf Goodman, known for rebranding Gucci and hiring designer Tom Ford.

Ellin Saltzman

Head of the Fashion Office at Bergdorf Goodman, Saks Fifth Avenue, and Macy's.

Andrew Goodman

Owner of the property located at 754 Fifth Avenue, the home of Bergdorf Goodman.

Don Eugene

Referred to as "Rabbi," a key figure in navigating internal audits and fraud investigations.

Mike Ullman

CEO during critical transitions and conversions at Macy's, known for pushing aggressive timelines.